Melody, Lyrics and Simplified Chords

100 Songs in **THE** the Key of "C"

THE EASY JAZZ STANDARDS FAKE BOOK

ISBN 978-1-4768-1315-8

HAL•LEONARD®
CORPORATION
7777 W. BLUEMOUND RD. P.O. BOX 13819 MILWAUKEE, WI 53213

Visit Hal Leonard Online at
www.halleonard.com

3 1800 00302 5182

THE EASY JAZZ STANDARDS FAKE BOOK

CONTENTS

INTRODUCTION

What Is a Fake Book?

A fake book has one-line music notation consisting of melody, lyrics and chord symbols. This lead sheet format is a "musical shorthand" which is an invaluable resource for all musicians—hobbyists to professionals.
Here's how *The Easy Jazz Standards Fake Book* differs from most standard fake books:

- All songs are in the key of C.

- Many of the melodies have been simplified.

- Only five basic chord types are used—major, minor, seventh, diminished and augmented.

- The music notation is larger for ease of reading.

In the event that you haven't used chord symbols to create accompaniment, or your experience is limited, a chord speller chart is included at the back of the book to help you get started.

Have fun!

ALICE IN WONDERLAND
from Walt Disney's ALICE IN WONDERLAND

Words by BOB HILLIARD
Music by SAMMY FAIN

ALL OR NOTHING AT ALL

Words by JACK LAWRENCE
Music by ARTHUR ALTMAN

call. _____ The kiss in your eyes, the

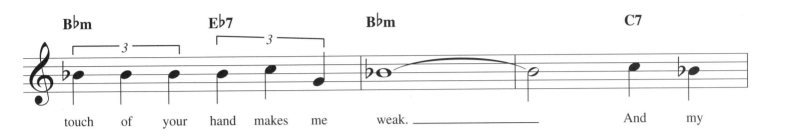

touch of your hand makes me weak. _____ And my

heart may grow diz - zy and fall. And if I

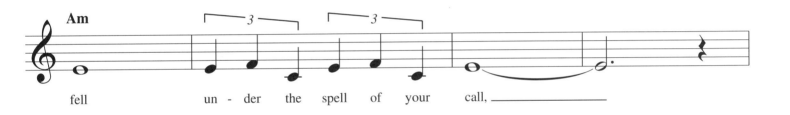

fell un - der the spell of your call, _____

I would be caught in the un - der - tow. _____

So, you see, I've got to say: No! No!

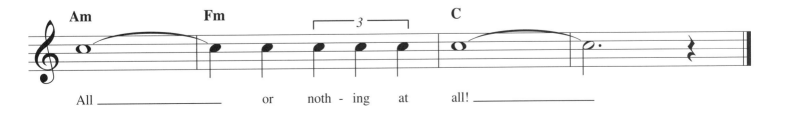

All _____ or noth - ing at all! _____

ALONE TOGETHER

Lyrics by HOWARD DIETZ
Music by ARTHUR SCHWARTZ

APRIL IN PARIS

Words by E.Y. "YIP" HARBURG
Music by VERNON DUKE

ALRIGHT, OKAY, YOU WIN

Words and Music by SID WYCHE
and MAYME WATTS

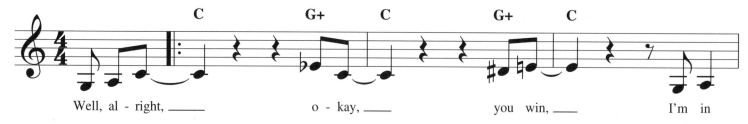

Well, al - right, _____ o - kay, _____ you win, _____ I'm in

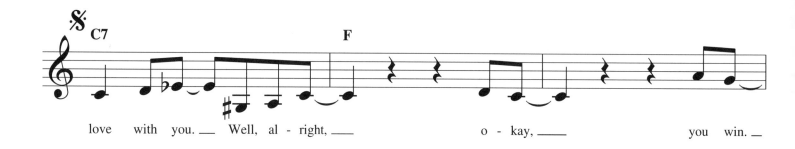

love with you. ___ Well, al - right, ___ o - kay, ___ you win. _

_____ Ba - by, what can I do? ___ I'll _____ do an - y - thing _ you say, _

_ {it's just got - ta be that way. ___
{as long as it's me and you. _   Well, al - right, ___

_____ All that ___ I am ask - in',

all I want ___ from you, ___ just love ___ me like

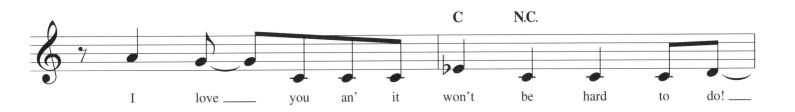

I love ___ you an' it won't be hard to do! ___

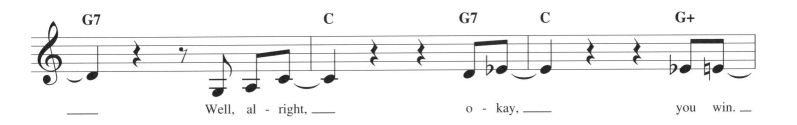

___ Well, al - right, ___ o - kay, ___ you win. ___

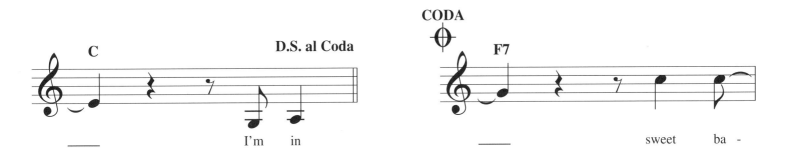

___ I'm in ___ sweet ba -

- by, take me by the hand. ___ Well, al - right, ___ o - kay, ___

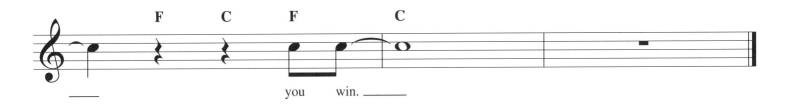

___ you win. _____

AT LAST

Lyric by MACK GORDON
Music by HARRY WARREN

BLUESETTE

Words by NORMAN GIMBEL
Music by JEAN THIELEMANS

Moderate Waltz

1. Poor lit - tle, sad lit - tle blue Blues - ette. Don't you
2., 3. Long as there's love in your heart to share, dear Blues -

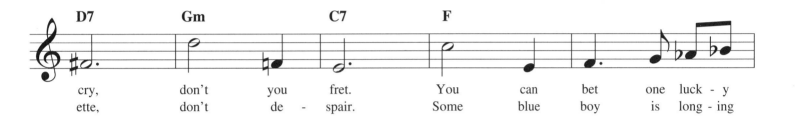

cry, don't you fret. You can bet one luck - y
ette, don't de - spair. Some blue boy is long - ing

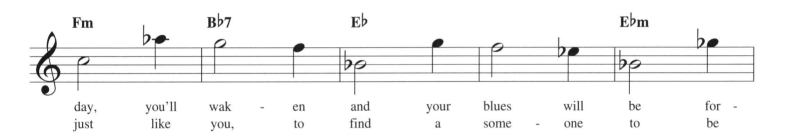

day, you'll wak - en and your blues will be for -
just like you, to find a some - one to be

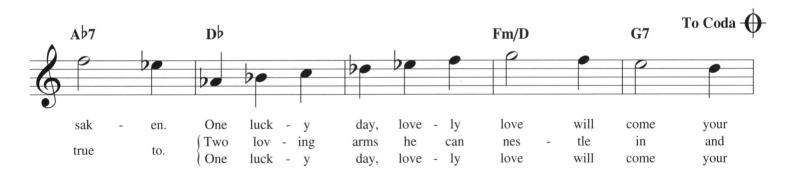

sak - en. One luck - y day, love - ly love will come your
true to. Two lov - ing arms he can nes - tle in and
One luck - y day, love - ly love will come your

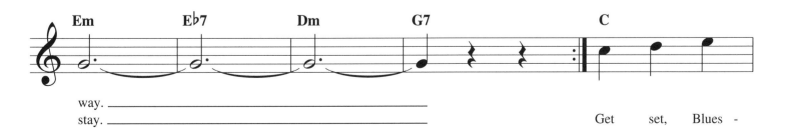

way. _____
stay. _____

Get set, Blues -

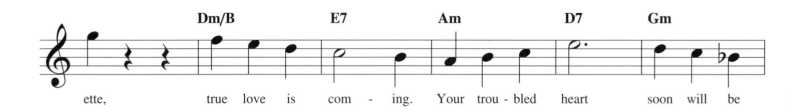

ette,   true love is   com - ing.   Your trou - bled   heart   soon   will   be

hum - ming.   *Hum* _____

_____   Doo - ya, Doo - ya, Doo - ya,

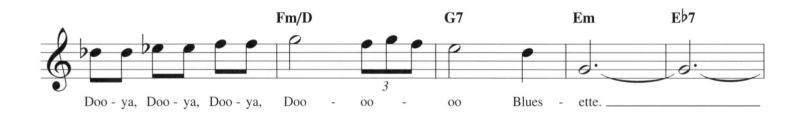

Doo - ya, Doo - ya, Doo - ya, Doo - oo - oo   Blues - ette. _____

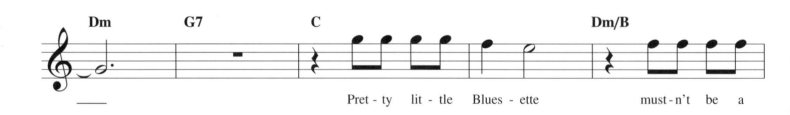

____   Pret - ty lit - tle Blues - ette   must - n't be a

mourn - er.   Have you heard the news   yet?   Love is 'round the

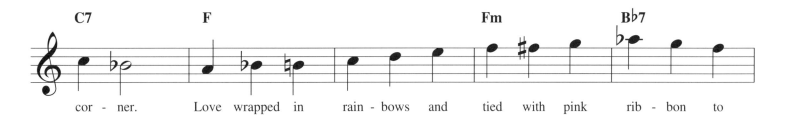

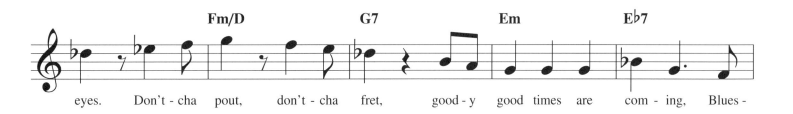

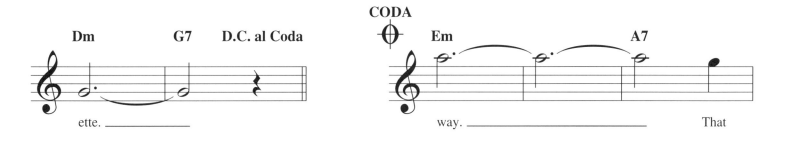

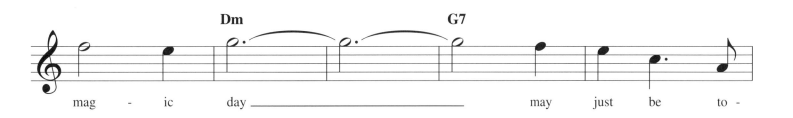

BEGIN THE BEGUINE
from JUBILEE

Words and Music by
COLE PORTER

When they be - gin _____ the Be - guine, _____ it

brings back the sound _____ of mu - sic so ten - der. _____ It

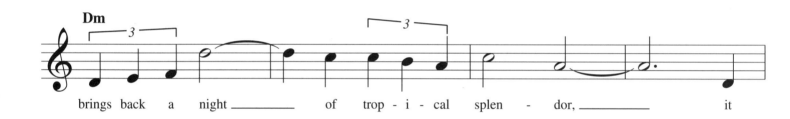

brings back a night _____ of trop - i - cal splen - dor, _____ it

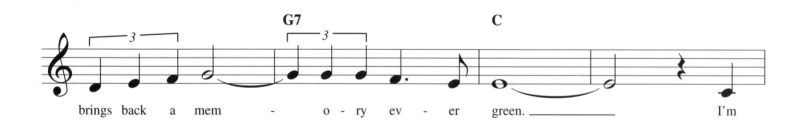

brings back a mem - o - ry ev - er green. _____ I'm

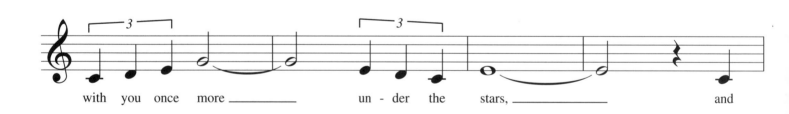

with you once more _____ un - der the stars, _____ and

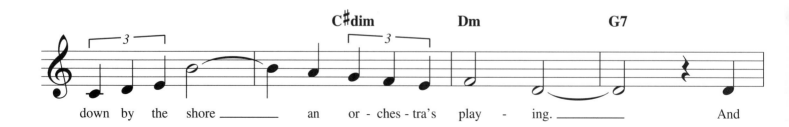

down by the shore _____ an or - ches - tra's play - ing. _____ And

BLUE MOON

Music by RICHARD RODGERS
Lyrics by LORENZ HART

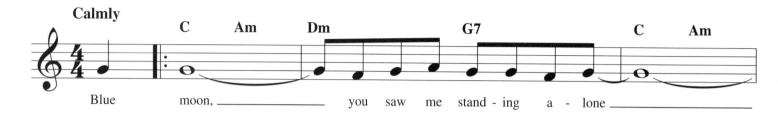

Blue moon, _____ you saw me stand-ing a - lone _____

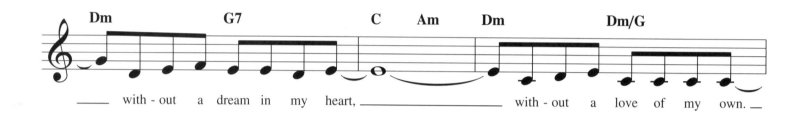

_____ with-out a dream in my heart, _____ with-out a love of my own. __

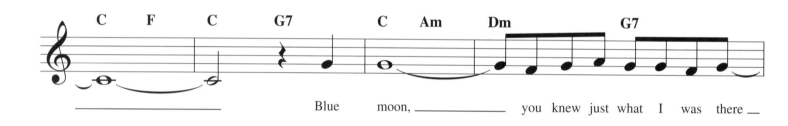

_____ Blue moon, _____ you knew just what I was there __

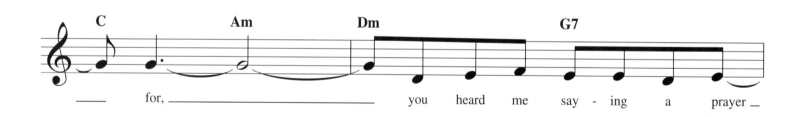

_____ for, _____ you heard me say - ing a prayer __

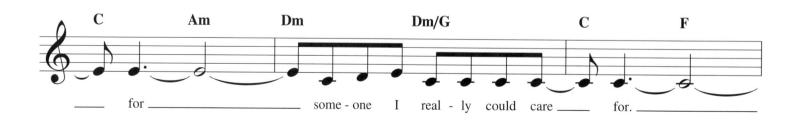

____ for _____ some - one I real - ly could care ___ for. _____

And then there sud-den-ly ap-peared be - fore me _____ the on - ly

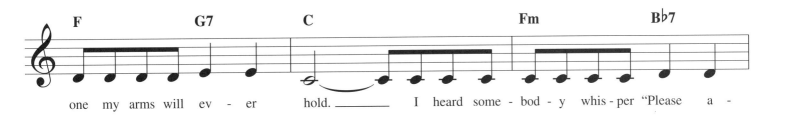

one my arms will ev - er hold. _____ I heard some-bod-y whis-per "Please a -

dore me" _____ and when I looked, the moon had turned to gold! Blue

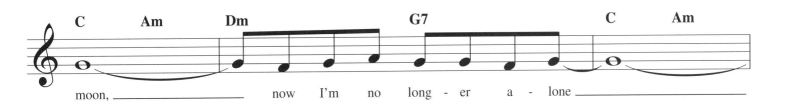

moon, _____ now I'm no long - er a - lone _____

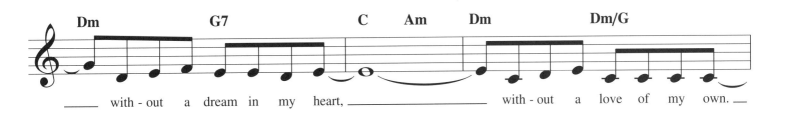

____ with - out a dream in my heart, _____ with - out a love of my own. ____

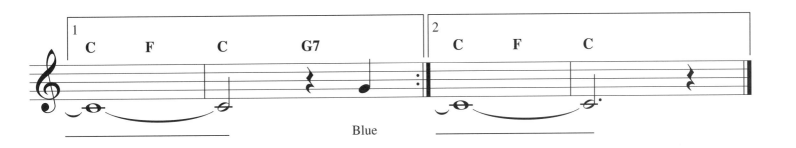

Blue

BODY AND SOUL

Words by EDWARD HEYMAN,
ROBERT SOUR and FRANK EYTON
Music by JOHN GREEN

Slow Ballad

My heart is sad and lone - ly,

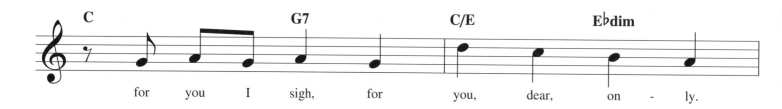

for you I sigh, for you, dear, on - ly.

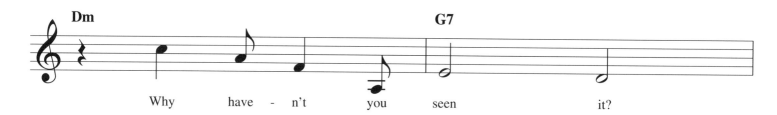

Why have - n't you seen it?

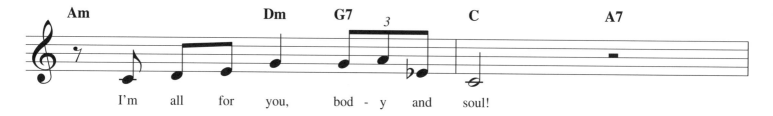

I'm all for you, bod - y and soul!

I spend my days in long - ing

and won - d'ring why it's me you're wrong - ing.

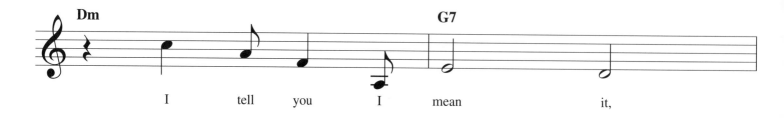

I tell you I mean it,

THE BOY NEXT DOOR
from MEET ME IN ST. LOUIS

Words and Music by HUGH MARTIN
and RALPH BLANE

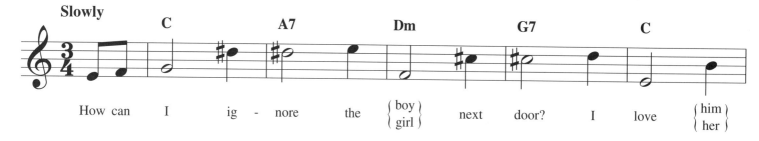

How can I ig - nore the {boy/girl} next door? I love {him/her}

more than I can say. ____ Does - n't try to please me,

does - n't e - ven tease me, and {he/she} nev - er sees me glance {his/her}

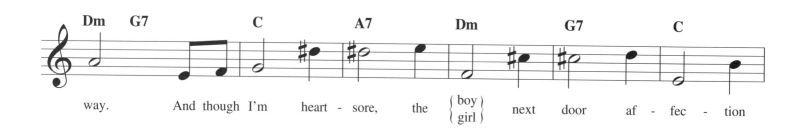

way. And though I'm heart - sore, the {boy/girl} next door af - fec - tion

for me won't dis - play. ____ I just a - dore {him/her} so I

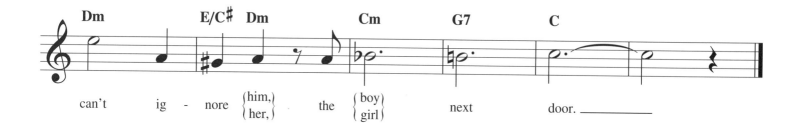

can't ig - nore {him,/her,} the {boy/girl} next door. ____

BUT NOT FOR ME
from GIRL CRAZY

Music and Lyrics by GEORGE GERSHWIN
and IRA GERSHWIN

CAST YOUR FATE TO THE WIND

Music by
VINCE GUARALDI

CHARADE
from CHARADE

Music by HENRY MANCINI
Words by JOHNNY MERCER

A CHILD IS BORN

Music by THAD JONES
Lyrics by ALEX WILDER

DARN THAT DREAM

Lyric by EDDIE DE LANGE
Music by JIMMY VAN HEUSEN

CRY ME A RIVER

Words and Music by
ARTHUR HAMILTON

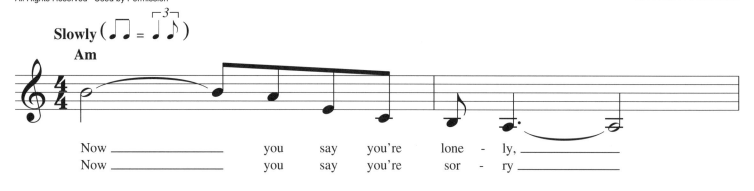

Now _____ you say you're lone - ly, _____
Now _____ you say you're sor - ry _____

you cry the long night thru; _____ } well, you can
for be - in' so un - true; _____

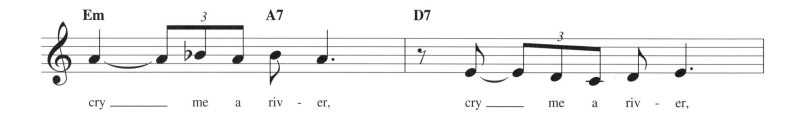

cry _____ me a riv - er, cry _____ me a riv - er,

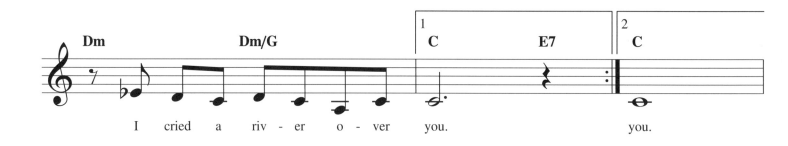

I cried a riv - er o - ver you.   you.

You drove me, ___ near-ly drove me out of my head, ___ while

you _____ nev - er shed a tear. _____

Re - mem - ber? ____ I re - mem - ber all that you said; ____

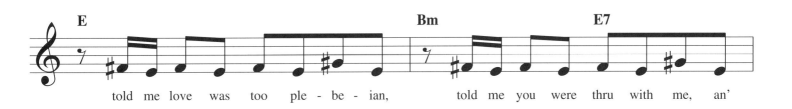

told me love was too ple - be - ian, told me you were thru with me, an'

now _____ you say you love me. _____

Well, just to prove you do, _____ come on, an'

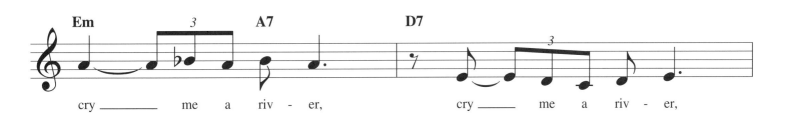

cry _____ me a riv - er, cry _____ me a riv - er,

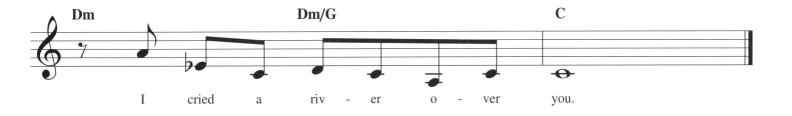

I cried a riv - er o - ver you.

DAY DREAM

Words by JOHN LATOUCHE
Music by DUKE ELLINGTON
and BILLY STRAYHORN

DAYS OF WINE AND ROSES
from DAYS OF WINE AND ROSES

Lyrics by JOHNNY MERCER
Music by HENRY MANCINI

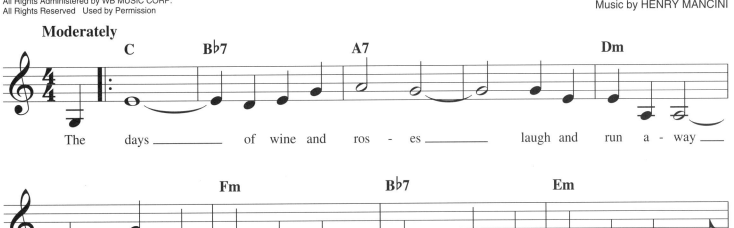

The days _____ of wine and ros - es _____ laugh and run a - way _____

_____ like a child at play, _____ through the mead - ow - land to -

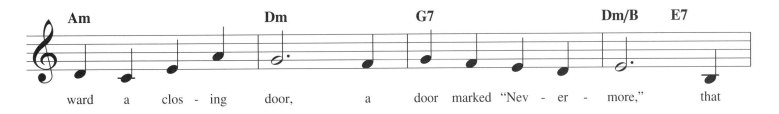

ward a clos - ing door, a door marked "Nev - er - more," that

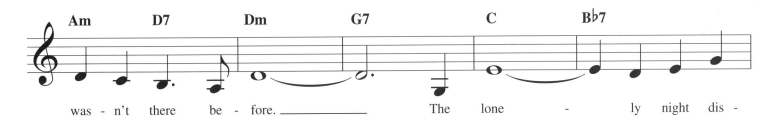

was - n't there be - fore. _____ The lone - ly night dis -

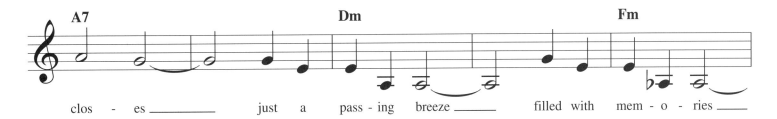

clos - es _____ just a pass - ing breeze _____ filled with mem - o - ries _____

_____ of the gold - en smile that in - tro - duced me to _____ the

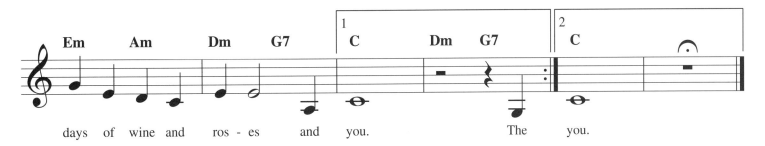

days of wine and ros - es and you. The you.

DEVIL MAY CARE

Words and Music by ROBERT DOROUGH
and TERRELL KIRK, JR.

No ___ cares for me; I'm ___ hap - py ___ as I can

be. I've learned to love and to live, dev - il may ___

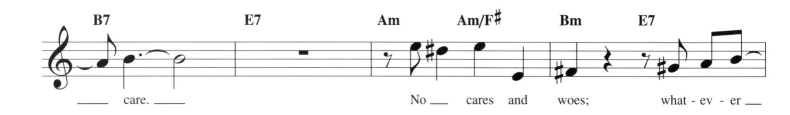

___ care. ___ No ___ cares and woes; what - ev - er ___

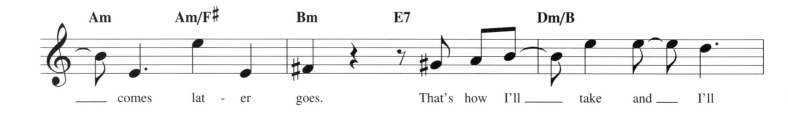

___ comes lat - er goes. That's how I'll ___ take and ___ I'll

give, dev - il may ___ care. ___ When the day is through,

I ___ suf - fer no re - grets. I know that

DON'T BLAME ME

Words by DOROTHY FIELDS
Music by JIMMY McHUGH

DREAM

Words and Music by
JOHNNY MERCER

Slowly

Dream _____ when you're feel - in' blue. _____

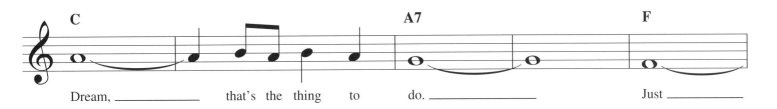

Dream, _____ that's the thing to do. _____ Just _____

____ watch the smoke rings rise in the air. _____ You'll find your share ____

____ of mem - o - ries there. _____ So dream _____

____ when the day is through. _____ Dream _____ and they might come

true. _____ Things _____ nev - er are as bad as they seem, ____

____ so dream, dream, dream. _____

EASY TO LOVE
(You'd Be So Easy to Love)
from BORN TO DANCE

Words and Music by
COLE PORTER

Easy Swing

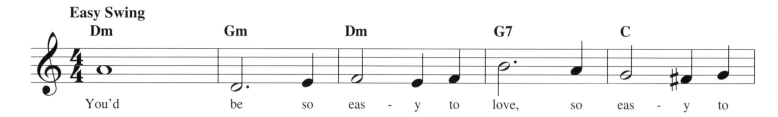

You'd   be so eas - y to love, so eas - y to

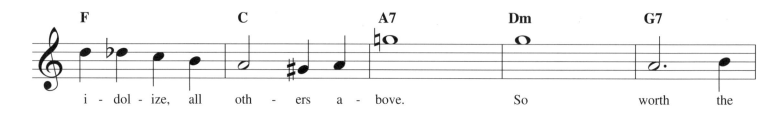

i - dol - ize, all oth - ers a - bove.   So   worth the

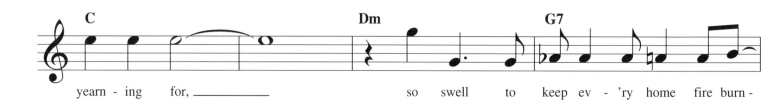

yearn - ing for, _____   so swell to keep ev - 'ry home fire burn -

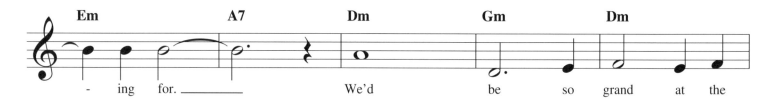

- ing for. _____   We'd   be so grand at the

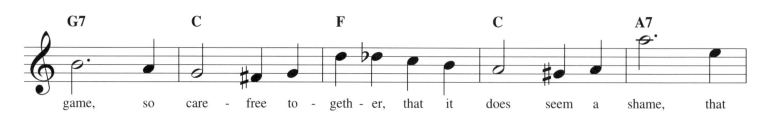

game,   so care - free to - geth - er, that it does seem a shame, that

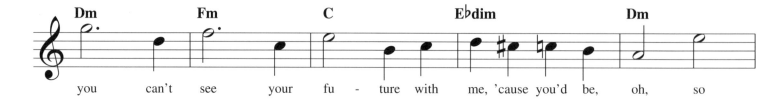

you can't see your fu - ture with me, 'cause you'd be, oh, so

eas - y to love! _____   love! _____

EMBRACEABLE YOU
from CRAZY FOR YOU

Music and Lyrics by GEORGE GERSHWIN
and IRA GERSHWIN

Whimsically

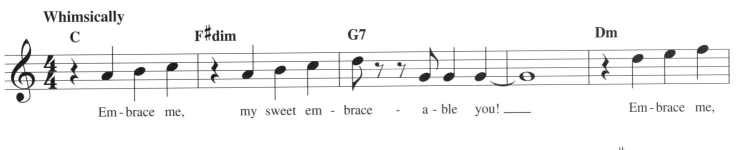

Em - brace me, my sweet em - brace - a - ble you! ___ Em - brace me,

you ir - re - place - a - ble you! ___ Just one look at you, my heart grew

tip - sy in me; ___ you and you a - lone bring out the gyp - sy in me! __

___ I love all the man - y charms a - bout you; ___

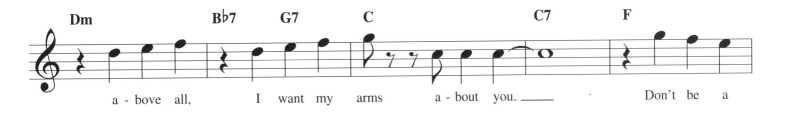

a - bove all, I want my arms a - bout you. ___ Don't be a

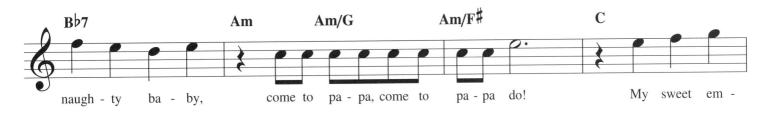

naugh - ty ba - by, come to pa - pa, come to pa - pa do! My sweet em -

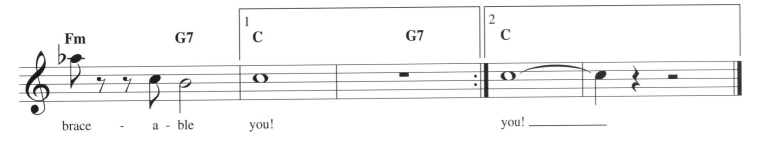

brace - a - ble you! you! ___

EMILY
from the MGM Motion Picture THE AMERICANIZATION OF EMILY

Music by JOHNNY MANDEL
Words by JOHNNY MERCER

Moderately slow

Em - i - ly, Em - i - ly, Em - i - ly _____ has the mur - mur - ing sound of

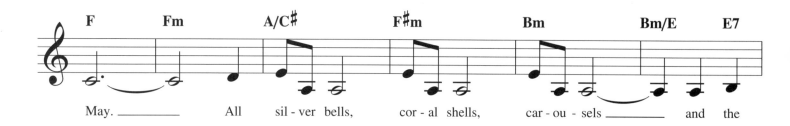

May. _____ All sil - ver bells, cor - al shells, car - ou - sels _____ and the

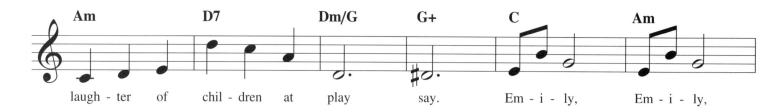

laugh - ter of chil - dren at play say. Em - i - ly, Em - i - ly,

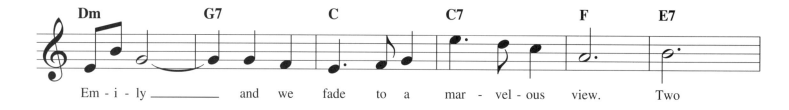

Em - i - ly _____ and we fade to a mar - vel - ous view. Two

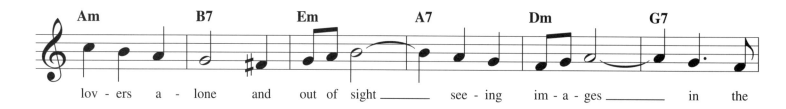

lov - ers a - lone and out of sight _____ see - ing im - a - ges _____ in the

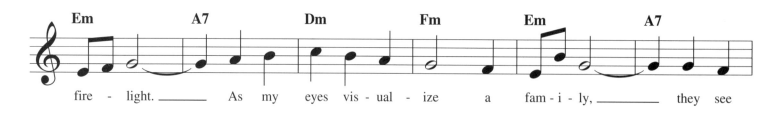

fire - light. _____ As my eyes vis - ual - ize a fam - i - ly, _____ they see

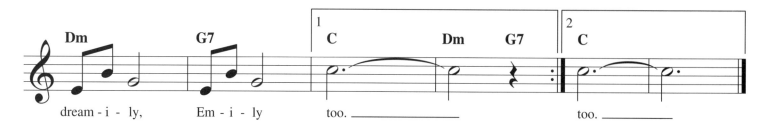

dream - i - ly, Em - i - ly   too. _____   too. _____

GOOD MORNING HEARTACHE

Words and Music by DAN FISHER,
IRENE HIGGINBOTHAM and ERVIN DRAKE

FASCINATING RHYTHM
from RHAPSODY IN BLUE

Music and Lyrics by GEORGE GERSHWIN
and IRA GERSHWIN

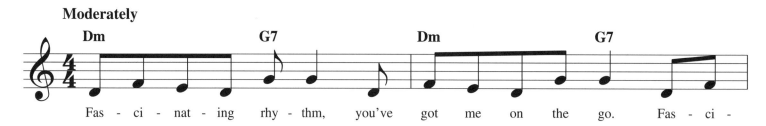

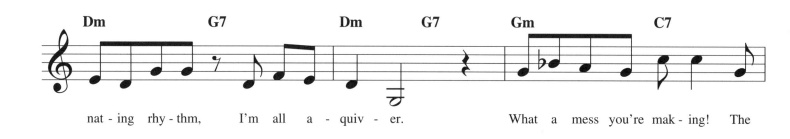

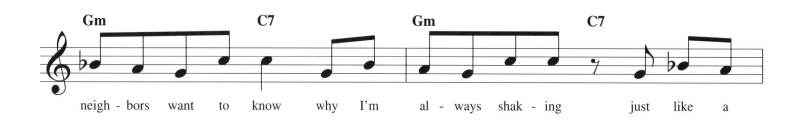

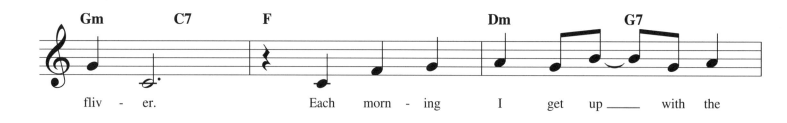

43

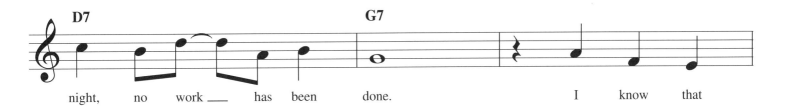

night, no work ___ has been done. I know that

once it did - n't mat - ter, but now you're do - ing wrong. When you

start to pat - ter, I'm so un - hap - py. Won't you take a day off? De -

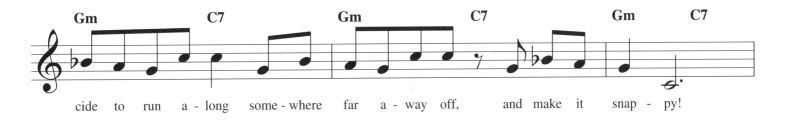

cide to run a - long some - where far a - way off, and make it snap - py!

Oh, how I long to be ___ the man I used to be!

Fas - ci - na - ting rhy - thm, oh, won't you stop pick - ing on me! _____

GENTLE RAIN
from the Motion Picture THE GENTLE RAIN

Music by LUIZ BONFA
Words by MATT DUBEY

Moderately

We _____ both are lost _____ and a - lone _____ in the

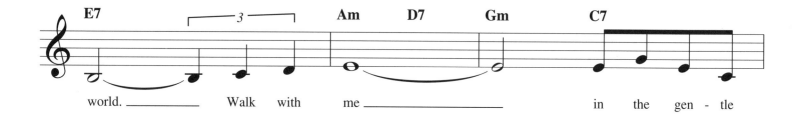

world. _____ Walk with me _____ in the gen - tle

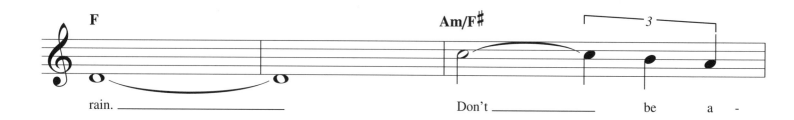

rain. _____ Don't _____ be a -

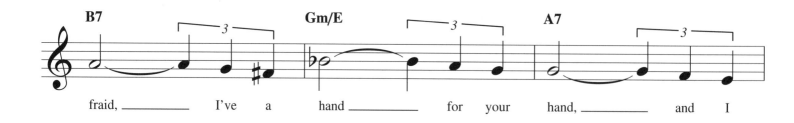

fraid, _____ I've a hand _____ for your hand, _____ and I

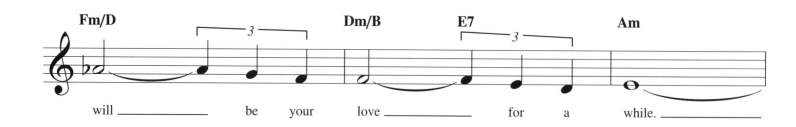

will _____ be your love _____ for a while. _____

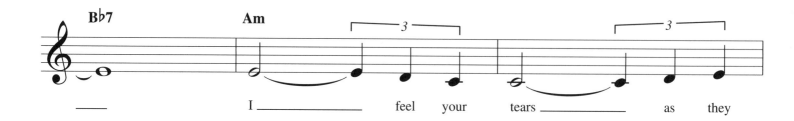

_____ I _____ feel your tears _____ as they

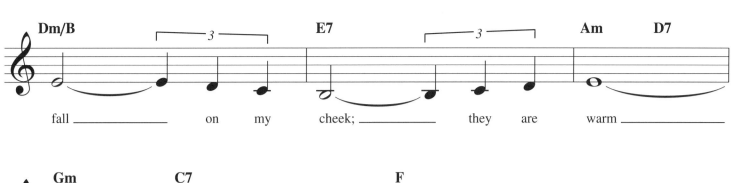

fall _____ on my cheek; _____ they are warm _____

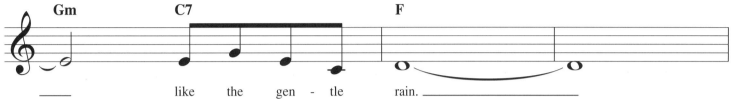

____ like the gen - tle rain. _____

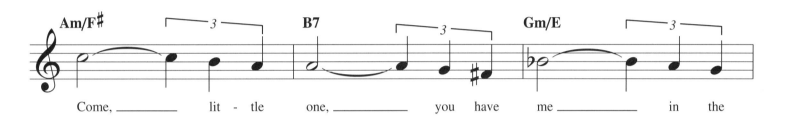

Come, _____ lit - tle one, _____ you have me _____ in the

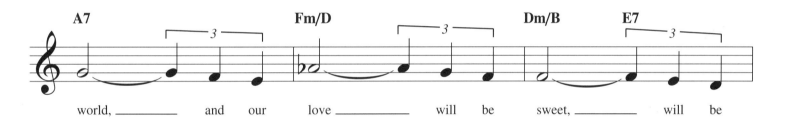

world, _____ and our love _____ will be sweet, _____ will be

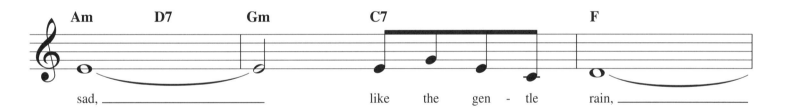

sad, _____ like the gen - tle rain, _____

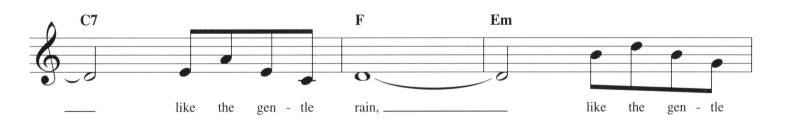

____ like the gen - tle rain, _____ like the gen - tle

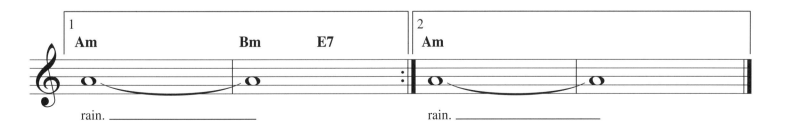

rain. _____   rain. _____

GIVE ME THE SIMPLE LIFE
from the Twentieth Century-Fox Picture WAKE UP AND DREAM

Words by HARRY RUBY
Music by RUBE BLOOM

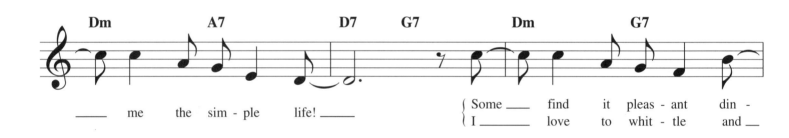

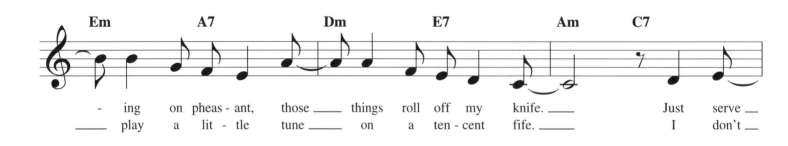

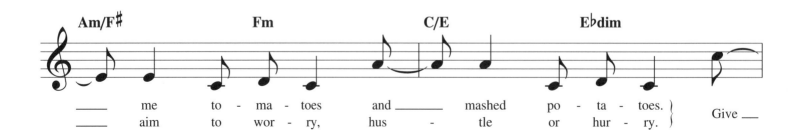

HARLEM NOCTURNE

Words by DICK ROGERS
Music by EARLE HAGEN

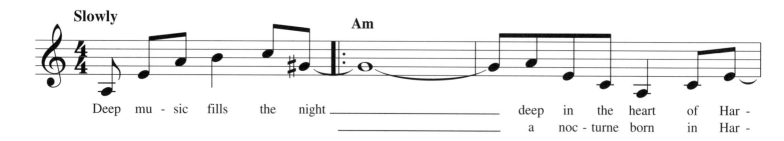

Deep mu - sic fills the night _____ deep in the heart of Har -
_____ a noc - turne born in Har -

- lem, _____ and tho' the stars are bright, _____
- lem; _____ that mel - an - chol - y strain _____

_____ the dark - ness is taunt - ing me. _____   Oh! what a sad re - frain, _
_____ for - ev - er is haunt - ing me. _

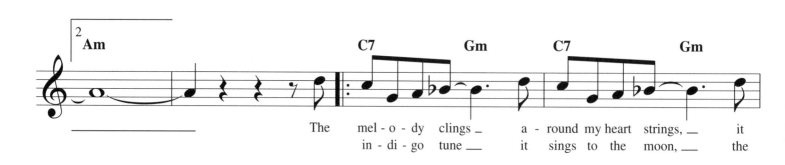

_____   The mel - o - dy clings _ a - round my heart strings, _ it
in - di - go tune _ it sings to the moon, _ the

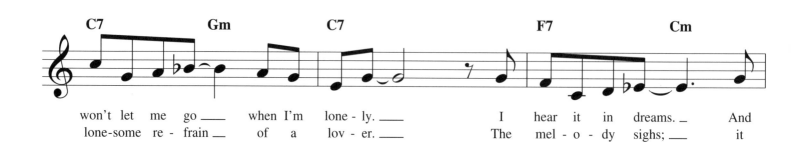

won't let me go _____ when I'm lone - ly. _____   I hear it in dreams. _ And
lone-some re - frain _ of a lov - er. _____   The mel - o - dy sighs; _____ it

49

some - how it seems ___ it makes ___ me ___ weep ___ and ___
laughs and it cries ___ a moan ___ in ___ blue ___ that ___

I ___ can't ___ sleep. An   wails ___ the ___ long ___ night ___ thru. ___

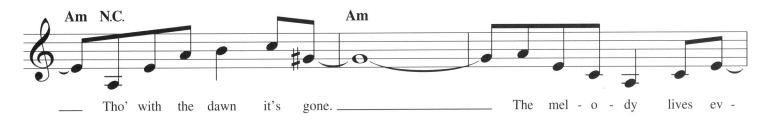

___ Tho' with the dawn it's gone. ___ The mel - o - dy lives ev -

- er ___ for lone - ly hearts to learn ___

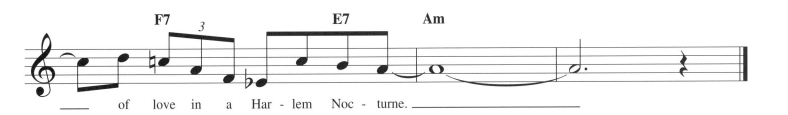

___ of love in a Har - lem Noc - turne. ___

HE LOVES AND SHE LOVES
from FUNNY FACE

Music and Lyrics by GEORGE GERSHWIN
and IRA GERSHWIN

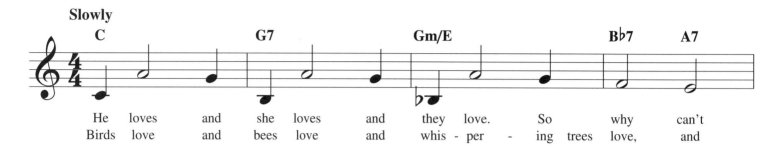

He loves and she loves and they love. So why can't
Birds love and bees love and whis - per - ing trees love, and

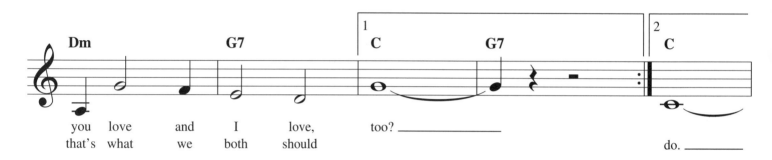

you love and I love, too? _____
that's what we both should

do. _____

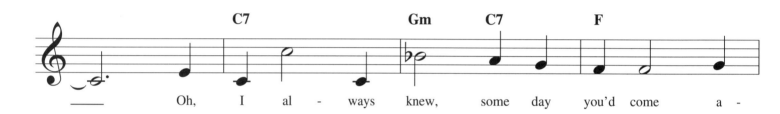

_____ Oh, I al - ways knew, some day you'd come a -

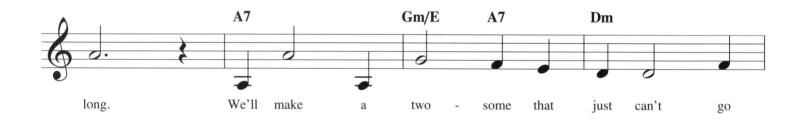

long. We'll make a two - some that just can't go

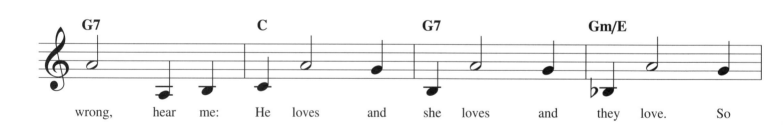

wrong, hear me: He loves and she loves and they love. So

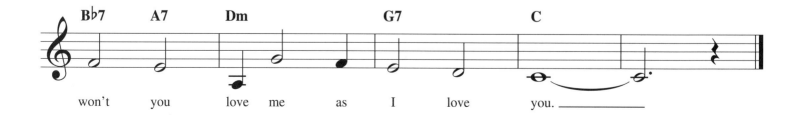

won't you love me as I love you. _____

HOW ABOUT YOU?

Words by RALPH FREED
Music by BURTON LANE

HEY THERE
from THE PAJAMA GAME

Words and Music by RICHARD ADLER
and JERRY ROSS

Slowly

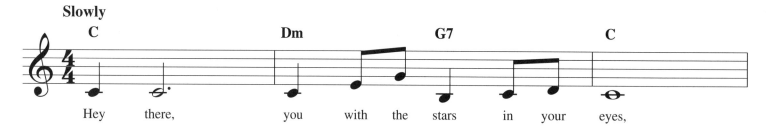

Hey there, you with the stars in your eyes,

love nev - er made a fool of you. You used to be too

wise! _____ Hey there, _____

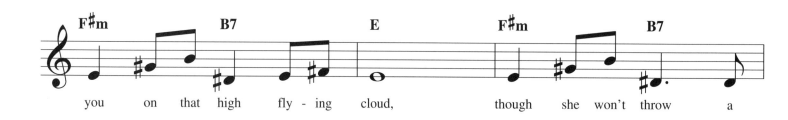

you on that high fly - ing cloud, though she won't throw a

crumb to you, you think some - day she'll come to you. _____

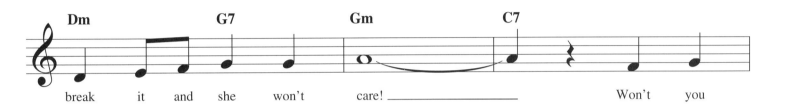

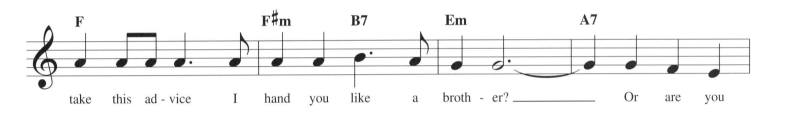

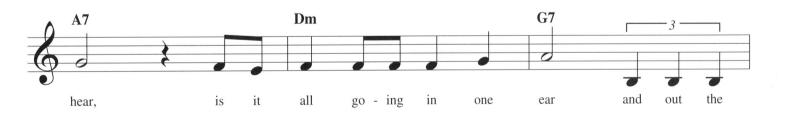

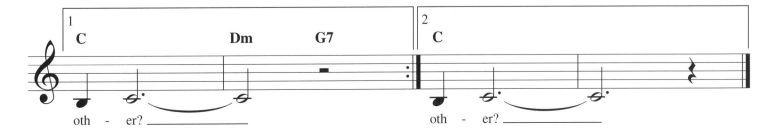

HOW LONG HAS THIS BEEN GOING ON?

Music and Lyrics by GEORGE GERSHWIN
and IRA GERSHWIN

I could cry ___ salt - y tears; ___ where have I been
I could cry ___ salt - y tears; ___ where have I been

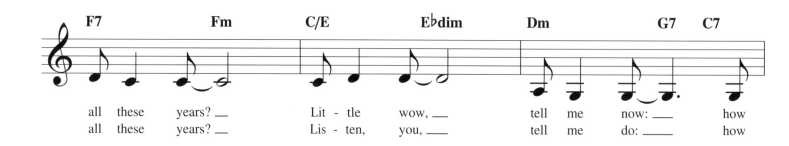

all these years? ___ Lit - tle wow, ___ tell me now: ___ how
all these years? ___ Lis - ten, you, ___ tell me do: ___ how

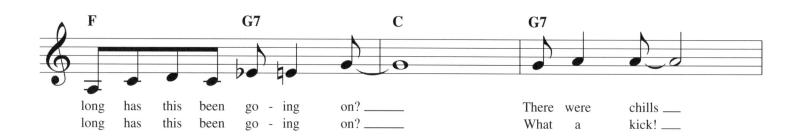

long has this been go - ing on? ___ There were chills ___
long has this been go - ing on? ___ What a kick! ___

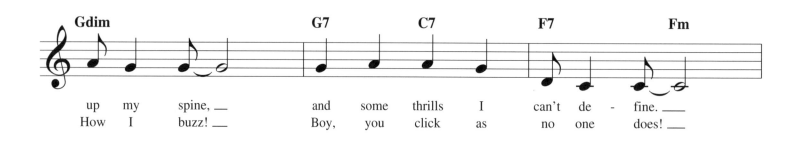

up my spine, ___ and some thrills I can't de - fine. ___
How I buzz! ___ Boy, you click as no one does! ___

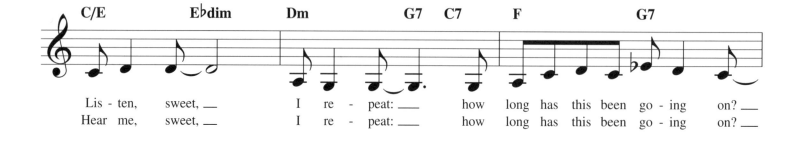

Lis - ten, sweet, ___ I re - peat: ___ how long has this been go - ing on? ___
Hear me, sweet, ___ I re - peat: ___ how long has this been go - ing on? ___

Oh, I feel that I could melt; ___
Dear, when in your arms I creep, ___

in - to heav - en I'm hurled. I know how Co -
that di - vine ren - dez - vous, don't wake me if

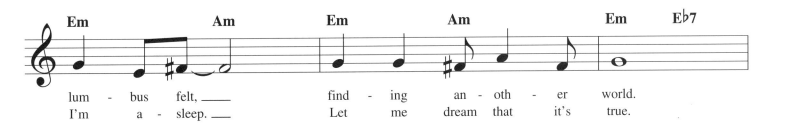

lum - bus felt, ___ find - ing an - oth - er world.
I'm a - sleep. ___ Let me dream that it's true.

Kiss me once, ___ then once more. ___ What a dunce I
Kiss me twice, ___ then once more. ___ That makes thrice; let's

was be - fore. ___) What a break! ___ For heav - en's sake! ___ How
make it four! ___)

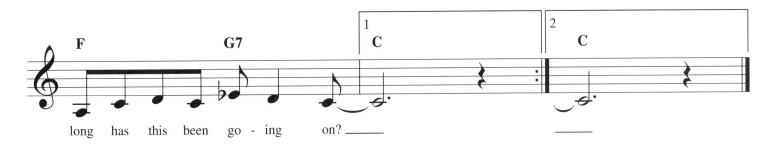

long has this been go - ing on? ___

I CAN DREAM, CAN'T I?
from RIGHT THIS WAY

Lyric by IRVING KAHAL
Music by SAMMY FAIN

I COULDN'T SLEEP A WINK LAST NIGHT

Words by HAROLD ADAMSON
Music by JIMMY McHUGH

I GET A KICK OUT OF YOU
from ANYTHING GOES

Words and Music by
COLE PORTER

I HAD THE CRAZIEST DREAM

Words by MACK GORDON
Music by HARRY WARREN

I MAY BE WRONG
(But I Think You're Wonderful!)

Words by HARRY RUSKIN
Music by HENRY SULLIVAN

I ONLY HAVE EYES FOR YOU

Words by AL DUBIN
Music by HARRY WARREN

I Want to Be Happy

Words by IRVING CAESAR
Music by VINCENT YOUMANS

Brightly

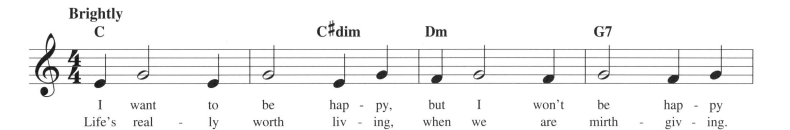

I want to be hap-py, but I won't be hap-py
Life's real-ly worth liv-ing, when we are mirth-giv-ing.

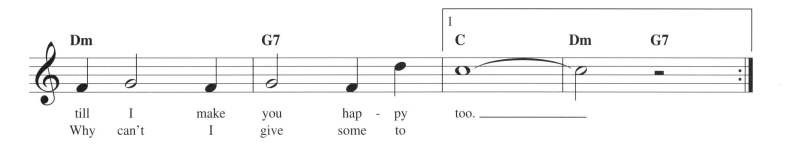

till I make you hap-py too.
Why can't I give some to

you?

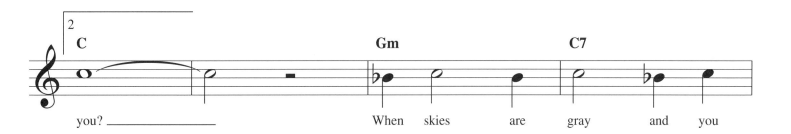

you? When skies are gray and you

say you are blue, I'll send the sun smil-ing through.

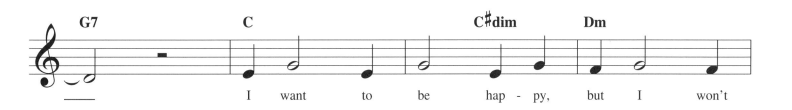

I want to be hap-py, but I won't

be hap-py till I make you hap-py too.

I THOUGHT ABOUT YOU

Words by JOHNNY MERCER
Music by JIMMY VAN HEUSEN

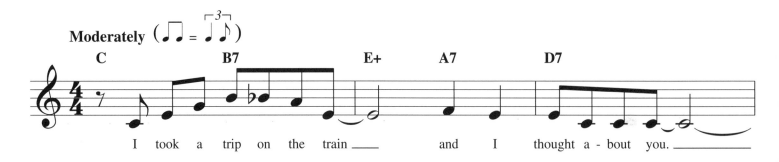

I took a trip on the train ___ and I thought a-bout you. ___

___ I passed a shad-ow-y lane ___ and I

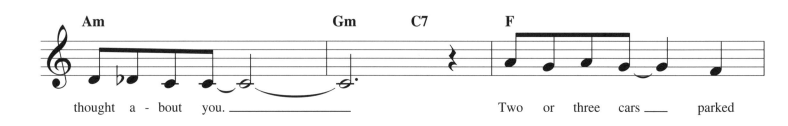

thought a-bout you. ___ Two or three cars ___ parked

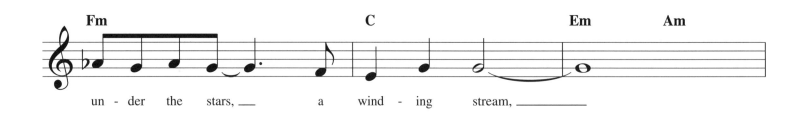

un-der the stars, ___ a wind-ing stream, ___

moon shin-ing down ___ on some lit-tle town, ___ and with each beam, ___

same old dream. ___ At ev - 'ry stop that we made, ___ oh, I

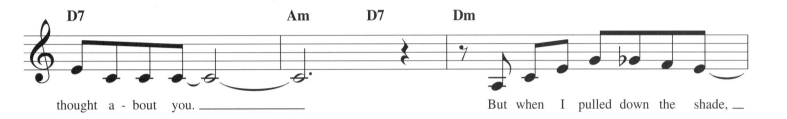

thought a - bout you. ___ But when I pulled down the shade, ___

___ then I real - ly felt blue. ___ I

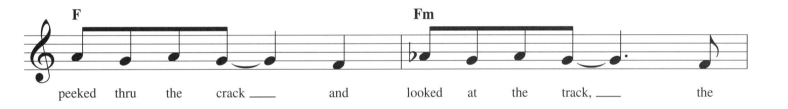

peeked thru the crack ___ and looked at the track, ___ the

one go - ing back ___ to you. And what did I do? ___

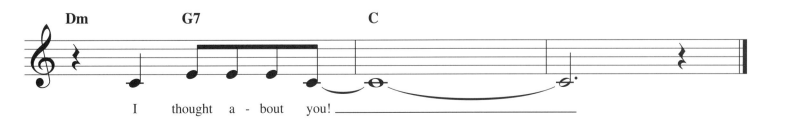

I thought a - bout you! ___

I WANNA BE AROUND

Words by JOHNNY MERCER
Music by SADIE VIMMERSTEDT

Moderately

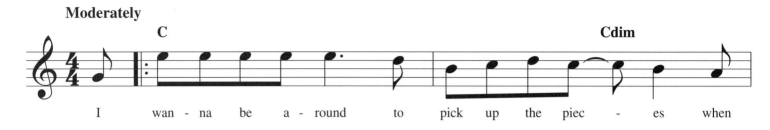

I wan - na be a - round to pick up the piec - es when

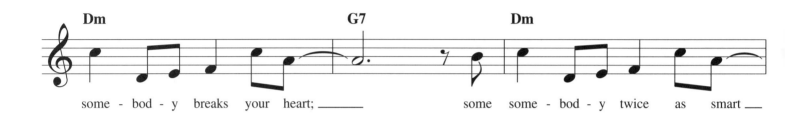

some - bod - y breaks your heart; _____ some some - bod - y twice as smart ____

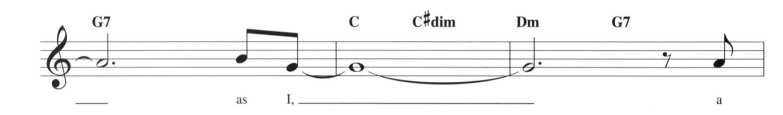

____ as I, _____ a

some - bod - y who ____ will swear to be true, ____ like

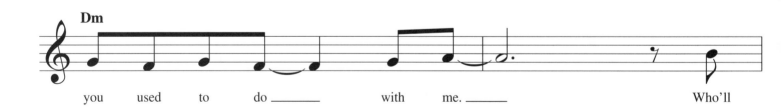

you used to do ____ with me. ____ Who'll

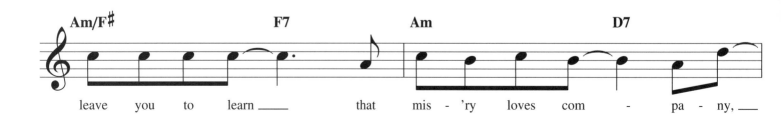

leave you to learn ____ that mis - 'ry loves com - pa - ny, ____

Dm   **G7**   **G+**   **C**

_____ wait and see! ____ I wan - na be a - round to

Cdim   **Dm**   **G7**

see how { he / she } does ___ it when { he / she } breaks your heart to bits; ____ let's

Dm   **G7**   **F7**   **E7**

see if the puz - zle fits _____ so fine. _____

A7

____ And that's when I'll dis - cov - er that re -

D7

venge is sweet; ___ as I sit here ap - plaud - ing from a

Dm

front row seat, ____ when some - bod - y breaks your heart like

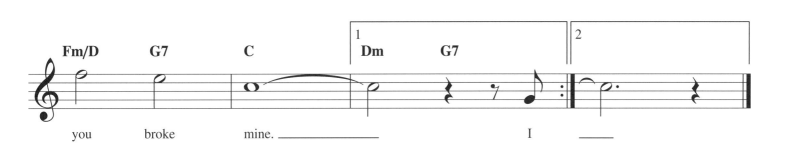

Fm/D   **G7**   **C** | 1 **Dm**   **G7** | 2

you broke mine. _____ I ___

I'LL STRING ALONG WITH YOU

Words by AL DUBIN
Music by HARRY WARREN

I'M IN THE MOOD FOR LOVE
from EVERY NIGHT AT EIGHT

Words and Music by JIMMY McHUGH
and DOROTHY FIELDS

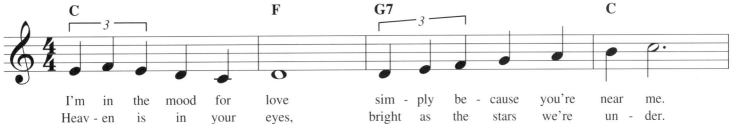

I'm in the mood for love, sim-ply be-cause you're near me.
Heav-en is in your eyes, bright as the stars we're un-der.

Fun-ny, but when you're near me, I'm in the mood for love.
Oh! Is it an-y won-der I'm in the mood for

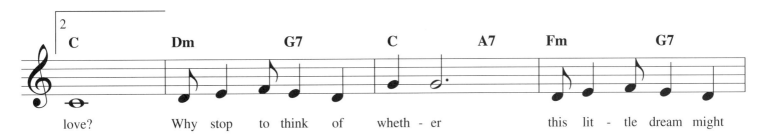

love? Why stop to think of wheth-er this lit-tle dream might

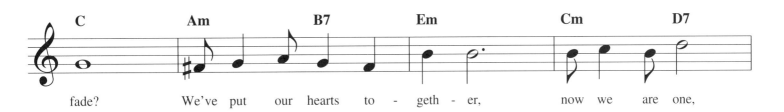

fade? We've put our hearts to-geth-er, now we are one,

I'm not a-fraid! If there's a cloud a-bove, if it should rain we'll

let it. But for to-night, for-get it! I'm in the mood for love.

I'M THRU WITH LOVE

Words by GUS KAHN
Music by MATT MALNECK and FUD LIVINGSTON

Moderately

I'm thru with love, I'll nev-er fall a-gain. Said "a-dieu" to love, "don't
locked my heart; I'll keep my feel-ings there. I have stocked my heart with

ev-er call a-gain," for I must have you or no one,
ic-y, frig-id air, and I need to care for no one,

and so I'm thru with love. I've
and so I'm thru with love.

Why did you lead me to think you could care? You did-n't need me, for

you had your share of slaves a-round you to hound you and swear with

deep e-mo-tion, de-vo-tion to you. Good-bye to spring, and

all it meant to me; it can nev-er bring the things that used to be, for I

must have you or no one, and so I'm thru with love.

IF I HAD YOU

Words and Music by TED SHAPIRO,
JIMMY CAMPBELL and REG CONNELLY

IF I RULED THE WORLD
from PICKWICK

Words by LESLIE BRICUSSE
Music by CYRIL ORNADEL

ILL WIND
(You're Blowin' Me No Good)
from COTTON CLUB PARADE

Lyric by TED KOEHLER
Music by HAROLD ARLEN

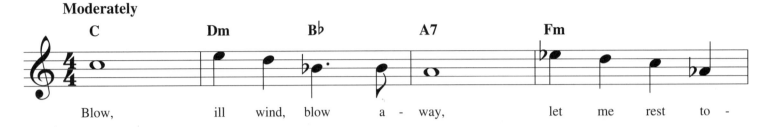

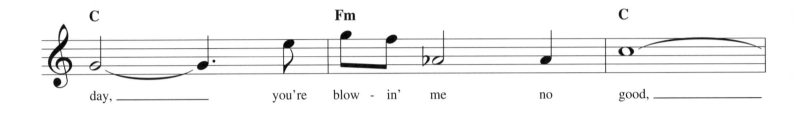

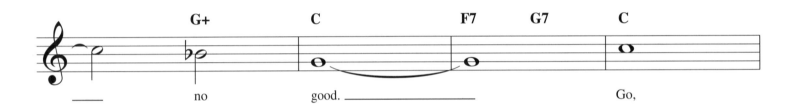

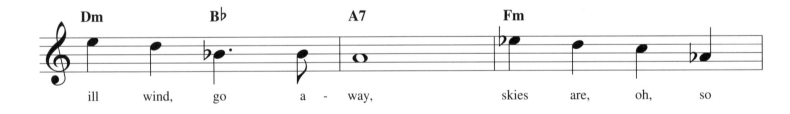

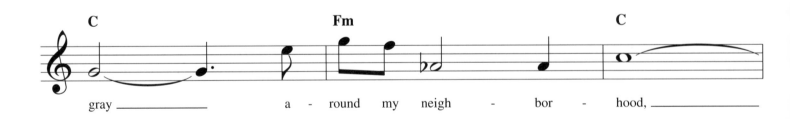

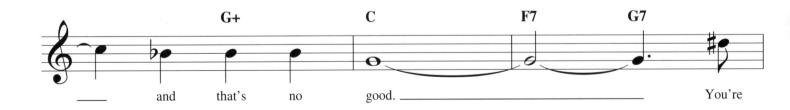

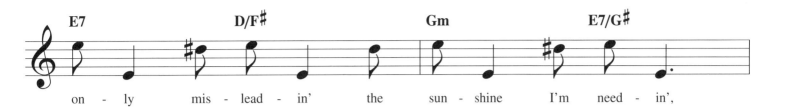

on - ly mis - lead - in' the sun - shine I'm need - in',

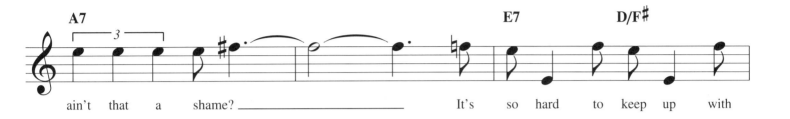

ain't that a shame? _____ It's so hard to keep up with

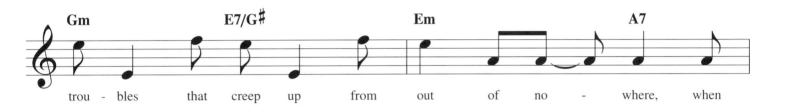

trou - bles that creep up from out of no - where, when

love's to blame. So, ill wind, blow a - way,

let me rest to - day, _____ you're blow - in' me no

good, _____ no good, _____

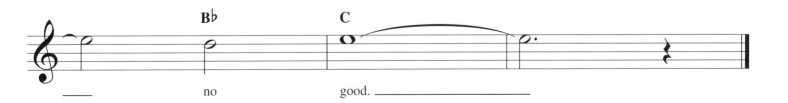

___ no good. _____

ISN'T IT A PITY?

Music and Lyrics by GEORGE GERSHWIN
and IRA GERSHWIN

Slowly

1., 3. It's a fun-ny thing;   I look at you,   I get a thrill
2., 4. Here we are at last!   It's like a dream!   The two of us,

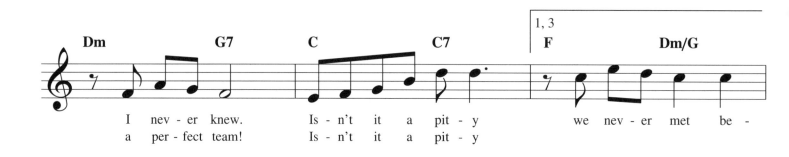

I nev-er knew.   Is-n't it a pit-y   we nev-er met be-
a per-fect team!   Is-n't it a pit-y

1, 3

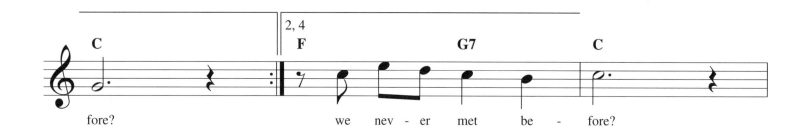

fore?

2, 4

we nev-er met be - fore?

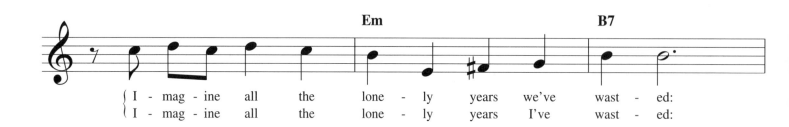

{ I - mag-ine all the lone - ly years we've wast - ed:
{ I - mag-ine all the lone - ly years I've wast - ed:

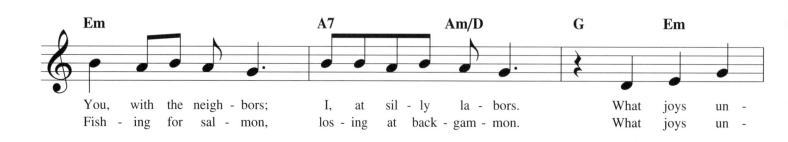

You, with the neigh-bors;   I, at sil-ly la-bors.   What joys un-
Fish-ing for sal-mon,   los-ing at back-gam-mon.   What joys un-

tast - ed! | You read - ing Hei - ne;
tast - ed! | My nights were sour _____

I, some - where in Chi - na. | Hap - pi - est of men
spent with Scho - pen - hau - er. | Let's for - get the past!

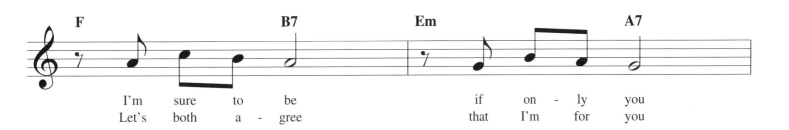

I'm sure to be | if on - ly you
Let's both a - gree | that I'm for you

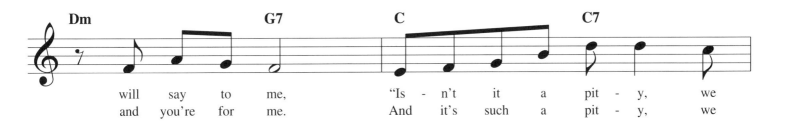

will say to me, | "Is - n't it a pit - y, we
and you're for me. | And it's such a pit - y, we

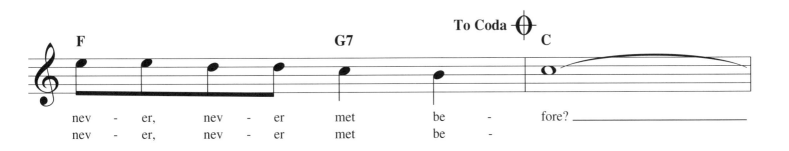

nev - er, nev - er met be - fore? _____
nev - er, nev - er met be -

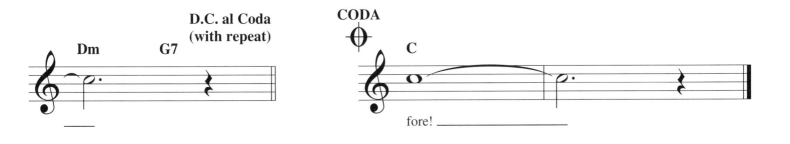

fore! _____

IT AIN'T NECESSARILY SO
from PORGY AND BESS

Music and Lyrics by GEORGE GERSHWIN,
DU BOSE and DOROTHY HEYWARD and IRA GERSHWIN

Moderately, with humor

It ain't ne-ces-sa-ri-ly so, it ain't ne-ces-sa-ri-ly
Da-vid was small, but oh my! Li'l Da-vid was small but oh

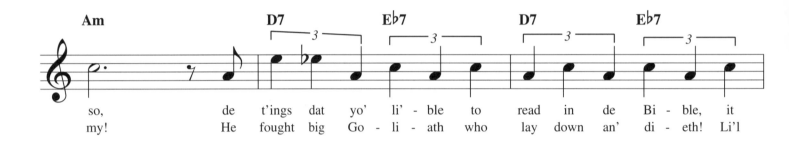

so, de t'ings dat yo' li-ble to read in de Bi-ble, it
my! He fought big Go-li-ath who lay down an' di-eth! Li'l

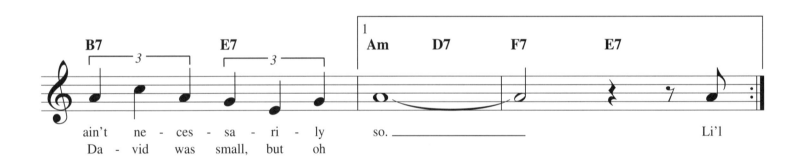

ain't ne-ces-sa-ri-ly so. Li'l
Da-vid was small, but oh

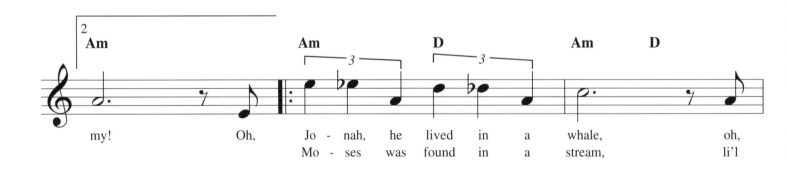

my! Oh, Jo-nah, he lived in a whale, oh,
Mo-ses was found in a stream, li'l

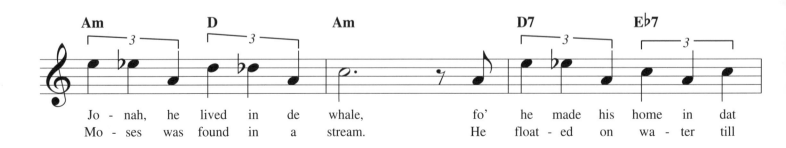

Jo-nah, he lived in de whale, fo' he made his home in dat
Mo-ses was found in a stream. He float-ed on wa-ter till

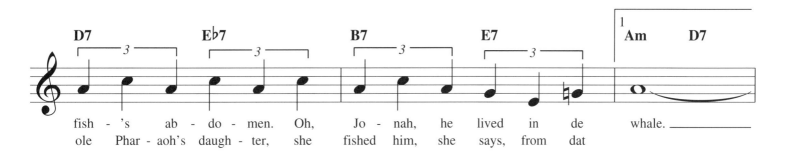

fish - 's ab - do - men. Oh, Jo - nah, he lived in de whale. _____
ole Phar - aoh's daugh - ter, she fished him, she says, from dat

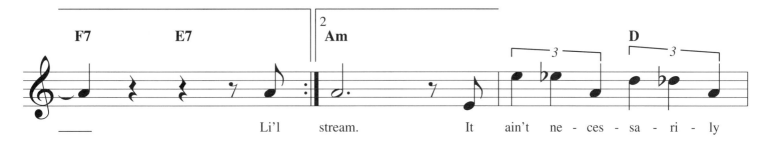

_____ Li'l stream. It ain't ne - ces - sa - ri - ly

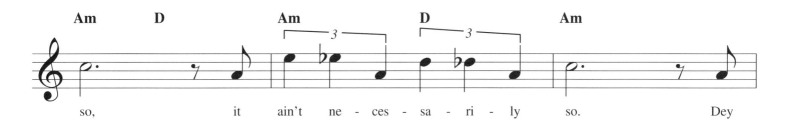

so, it ain't ne - ces - sa - ri - ly so. Dey

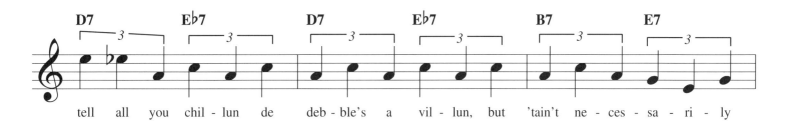

tell all you chil - lun de deb - ble's a vil - lun, but 'tain't ne - ces - sa - ri - ly

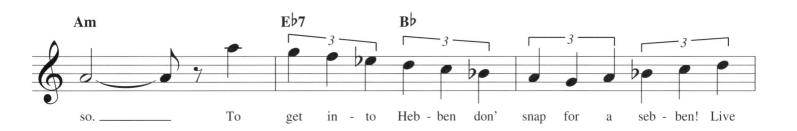

so. _____ To get in - to Heb - ben don' snap for a seb - ben! Live

clean! Don't have no fault. Oh, I takes dat gos - pel when -

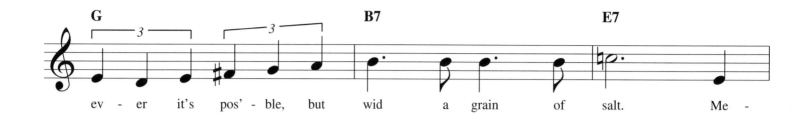

ev - er it's pos' - ble, but wid a grain of salt. Me -

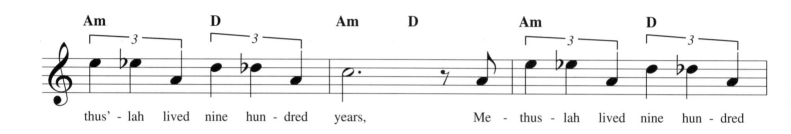

thus' - lah lived nine hun - dred years, Me - thus - lah lived nine hun - dred

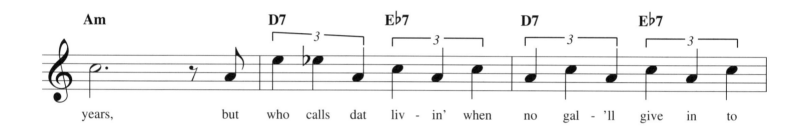

years, but who calls dat liv - in' when no gal - 'll give in to

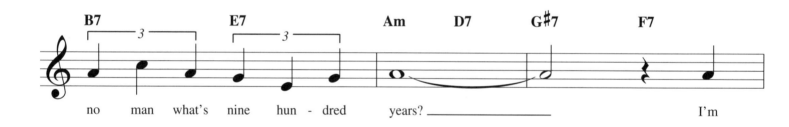

no man what's nine hun - dred years? _____ I'm

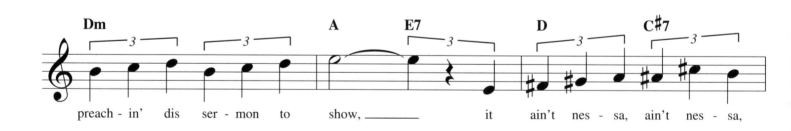

preach - in' dis ser - mon to show, _____ it ain't nes - sa, ain't nes - sa,

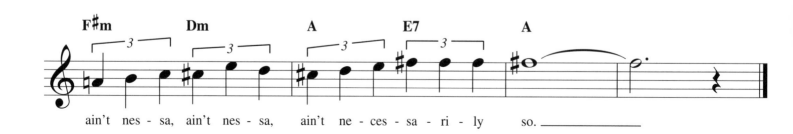

ain't nes - sa, ain't nes - sa, ain't ne - ces - sa - ri - ly so. _____

JUST FRIENDS

Lyrics by SAM M. LEWIS
Music by JOHN KLENNER

IT HAD TO BE YOU

Lyric by GUS KAHN
Music by ISHAM JONES

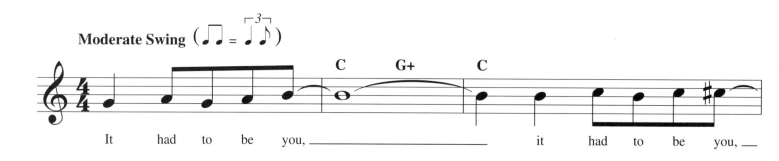

It had to be you, _____ it had to be you, __

_____ I wan-dered a-round __ and fi-nal-ly found __

__ the some-bod-y who _____ could make me be true,

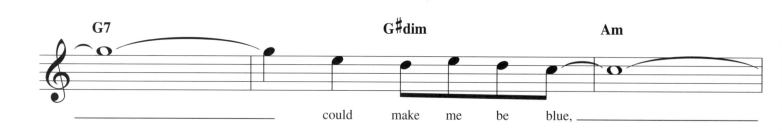

__ could make me be blue, _____

__ and e-ven be glad __ just to be sad, __ think-ing of you. __

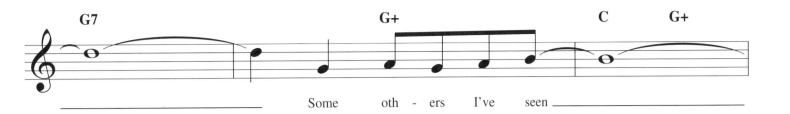

Some oth - ers I've seen

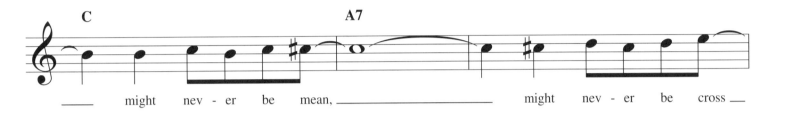

might nev - er be mean, might nev - er be cross

or try to be boss, but they would - n't do.

For no - bod - y else gave me a thrill, with all your faults

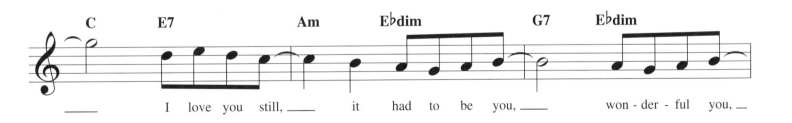

I love you still, it had to be you, won - der - ful you,

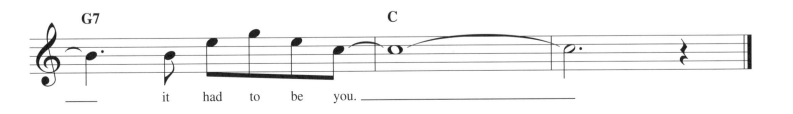

it had to be you.

JUST ONE OF THOSE THINGS
from HIGH SOCIETY

Words and Music by
COLE PORTER

Moderately

It was just one _____ of those things, _____

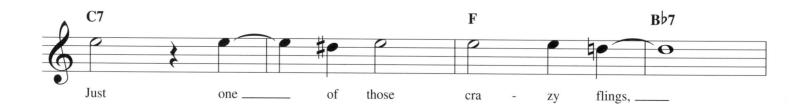

Just one _____ of those cra - zy flings, _____

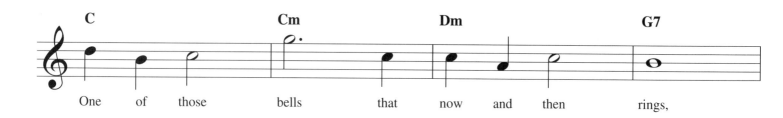

One of those bells that now and then rings,

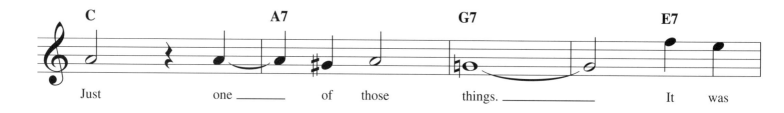

Just one _____ of those things. _____ It was

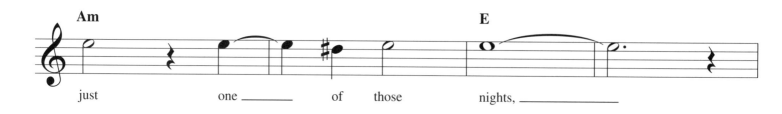

just one _____ of those nights, _____

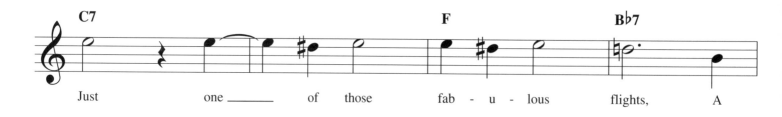

Just one _____ of those fab - u - lous flights, A

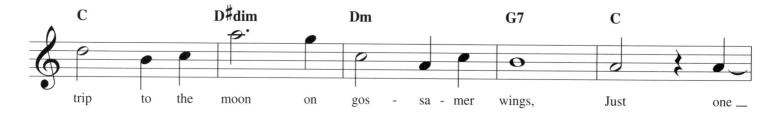

trip to the moon on gos - sa - mer wings, Just one _____

A KISS TO BUILD A DREAM ON

Words and Music by BERT KALMAR,
HARRY RUBY and OSCAR HAMMERSTEIN II

LAURA

Words by JOHNNY MERCER
Music by DAVID RAKSIN

LAZY AFTERNOON
from THE GOLDEN APPLE

Words and Music by JOHN LATOUCHE
and JEROME MOROSS

It's a la - zy af - ter - noon, and the

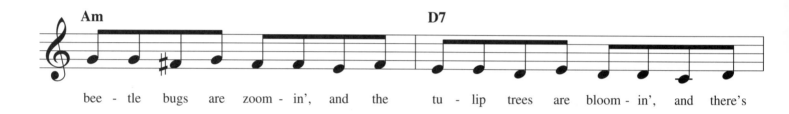

bee - tle bugs are zoom - in', and the tu - lip trees are bloom - in', and there's

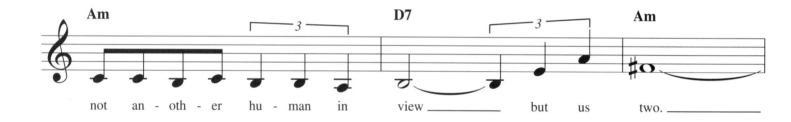

not an - oth - er hu - man in view _____ but us two. _____

_____ It's a la - zy af - ter - noon, and the

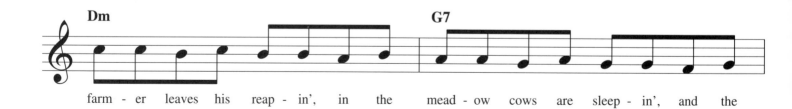

farm - er leaves his reap - in', in the mead - ow cows are sleep - in', and the

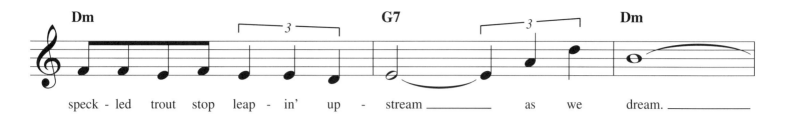

speck - led trout stop leap - in' up - stream _____ as we dream. _____

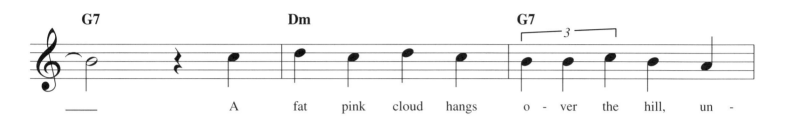

_____ A fat pink cloud hangs o - ver the hill, un -

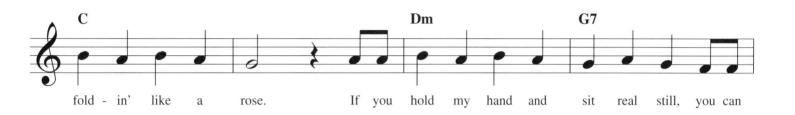

fold - in' like a rose. If you hold my hand and sit real still, you can

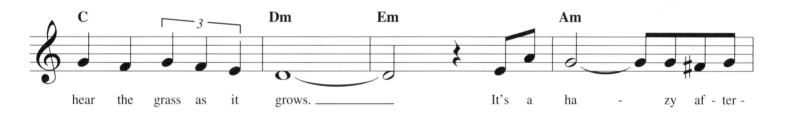

hear the grass as it grows. _____ It's a ha - zy af - ter -

noon, and I know a place that's qui - et 'cept for dai - sies run - ning ri - ot, and there's

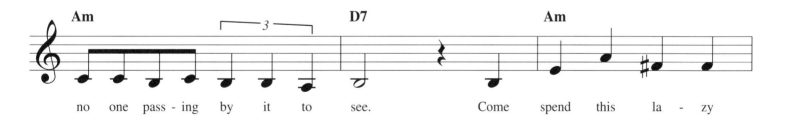

no one pass - ing by it to see. Come spend this la - zy

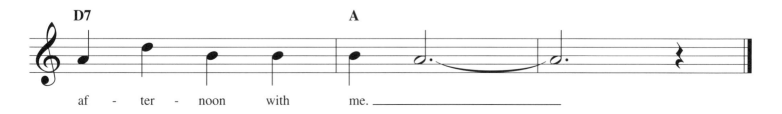

af - ter - noon with me. _____

LAZYBONES

Words and Music by HOAGY CARMICHAEL
and JOHNNY MERCER

LOVE IS HERE TO STAY

from GOLDWYN FOLLIES
from AN AMERICAN IN PARIS

Music and Lyrics by GEORGE GERSHWIN
and IRA GERSHWIN

It's ver - y clear our love is here to stay;

not for a year, but ev - er and a day. The ra - di -

o and the tel - e - phone and the mov - ies that we know may just be

pass - ing fan - cies, and in time may go. But oh, my

dear, our love is here to stay; to - geth - er

we're go - ing a long, long way. In time the

Rock - ies may crum - ble, Gi - bral - tar may tum - ble; they're on - ly made of

clay, but our love is here to stay.

LET'S CALL THE WHOLE THING OFF
from SHALL WE DANCE

Music and Lyrics by GEORGE GERSHWIN
and IRA GERSHWIN

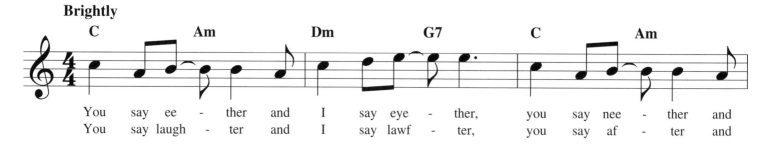

You say ee - ther and I say eye - ther, you say nee - ther and
You say laugh - ter and I say lawf - ter, you say af - ter and

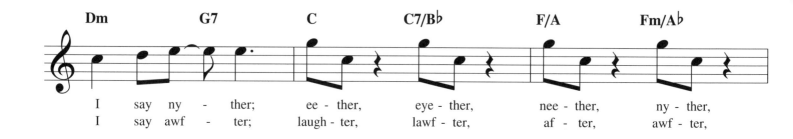

I say ny - ther; ee - ther, eye - ther, nee - ther, ny - ther,
I say awf - ter; laugh - ter, lawf - ter, af - ter, awf - ter,

let's call the whole thing off! You like po - ta - to and
let's call the whole thing off! You like va - nil - la and

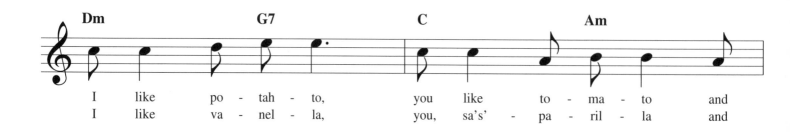

I like po - tah - to, you like to - ma - to and
I like va - nel - la, you, sa's' - pa - ril - la and

I like to - mah - to; po - ta - to, po - tah - to, to -
I sa's' - pa - rel - la; va - nil - la, va - nel - la, _____

LET'S DO IT
(Let's Fall in Love)
from PARIS

Words and Music by
COLE PORTER

Moderately

Birds   do   it, _____   bees   do   it, _____   e - ven ed - u - cat - ed
spon - ges, they _____ say,   do   it, _____   oys - ters down in Oys - ter

fleas   do   it. _____ } Let's   do   it, _____ let's   fall   in _____
Bay   do   it. _____ }

love. _____ { In   Spain,   the   best   up - per _____
                          { Cold   Cape   Cod   clams,   'gainst their _____

sets   do   it, _____   Lith - u - a - ni - ans and Letts do   it. _____ }
wish,   do   it, _____   e - ven la - zy jel - ly - fish do   it. _____ }

Let's   do   it, _____ let's   fall   in _____   love. _____

The Dutch in old Am - ster - dam do it, _____
E - lec - tric eels, I might _ add, do it, _____

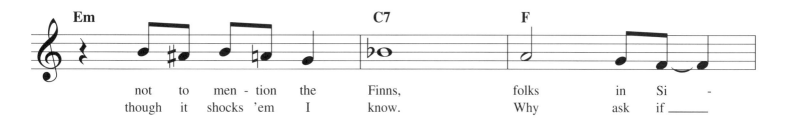

not to men - tion the Finns, folks in Si -
though it shocks 'em I know. Why ask if _____

am do it, _____ think of Si - a - mese twins. Some Ar - gen -
shad do it; _____ wait - er, bring me shad roe. In shal - low

tines, with - out _____ means, do it. _____ Peo - ple say, in Bos - ton, e - ven
shoals, Eng - lish _____ soles do it. _____ Gold - fish, in the pri - va - cy of

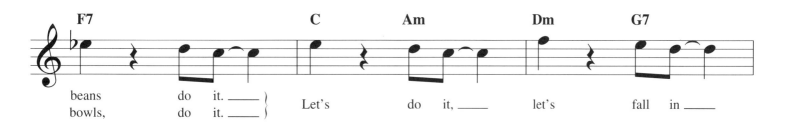

beans do it. _____ } Let's do it, _____ let's fall in _____
bowls, do it. _____ }

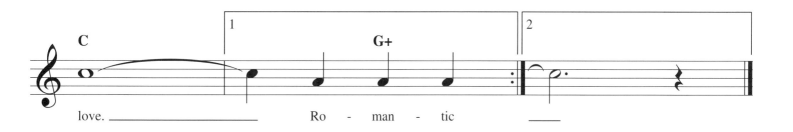

love. _____ Ro - man - tic _____

LOLLIPOPS AND ROSES

Words and Music by
TONY VELONA

With movement

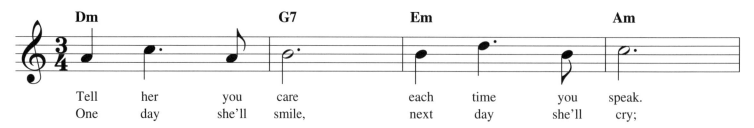

Tell her you care each time you speak.
One day she'll smile, next day she'll cry;

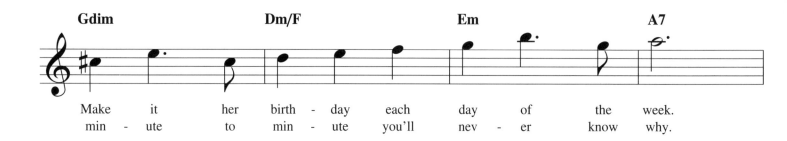

Make it her birth - day each day of the week.
min - ute to min - ute you'll nev - er know why.

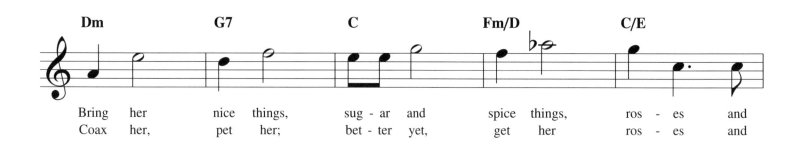

Bring her nice things, sug - ar and spice things, ros - es and
Coax her, pet her; bet - ter yet, get her ros - es and

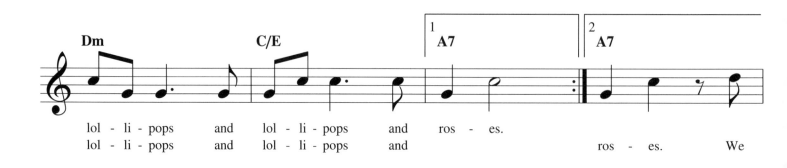

lol - li - pops and lol - li - pops and ros - es.
lol - li - pops and lol - li - pops and ros - es. We

try _____ act - ing grown - up, _____ but _____

____ as a rule _____ we're all _____ lit - tle

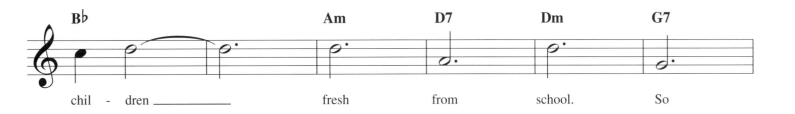

chil - dren _____ fresh from school. So

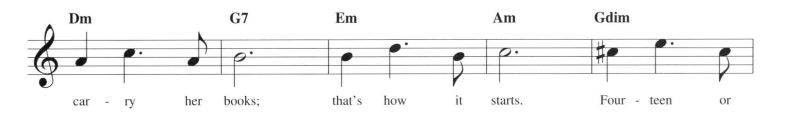

car - ry her books; that's how it starts. Four - teen or

for - ty, they're kids in their hearts. Keep them hand - y,

flow - ers and can - dy, ros - es and lol - li - pops and lol - li - pops ____

____ and ros - es. _____

LOVE FOR SALE
from THE NEW YORKERS

Words and Music by
COLE PORTER

Moderately fast

Love _____ for sale, _____

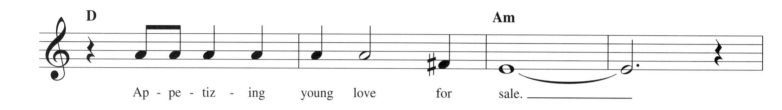

Ap - pe - tiz - ing young love for sale. _____

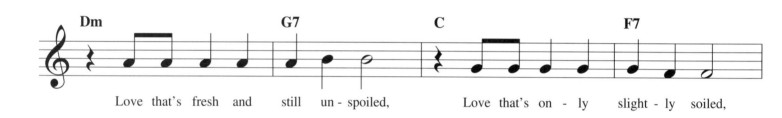

Love that's fresh and still un - spoiled, Love that's on - ly slight - ly soiled,

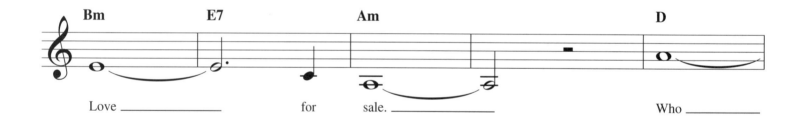

Love _____ for sale. _____ Who _____

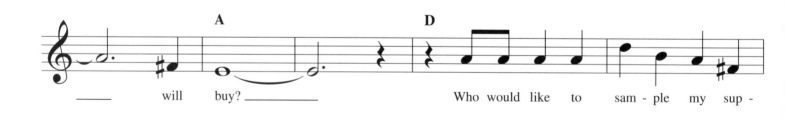

_____ will buy? _____ Who would like to sam - ple my sup -

ply? _____ Who's pre - pared to pay the price

99

LOVE LETTERS
Theme from the Paramount Picture LOVE LETTERS

Words by EDWARD HEYMAN
Music by VICTOR YOUNG

Love let-ters straight from your heart, _____ keep us so

near _____ while a-part. _____ I'm not a-lone _____ in the

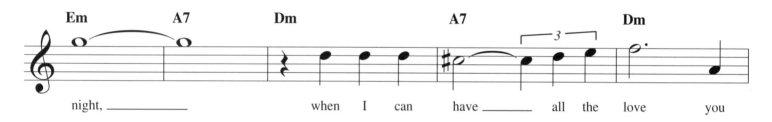

night, _____ when I can have _____ all the love you

write. I mem-o-rize ev-'ry line, _____

I kiss the name _____ that you sign. _____

And dar-ling, then I read a-gain right from the start

love let-ters straight from your heart. _____

LOVE WALKED IN

Music and Lyrics by GEORGE GERSHWIN
and IRA GERSHWIN

Moderately

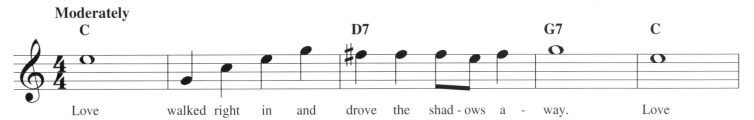

Love walked right in and drove the shad-ows a - way. Love

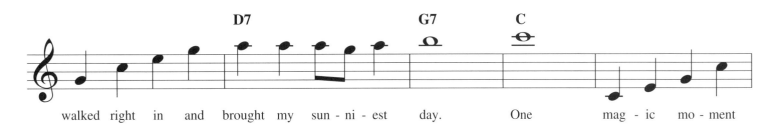

walked right in and brought my sun-ni-est day. One mag - ic mo - ment

and my heart seemed to know _____ that love said "Hel - lo," though not a

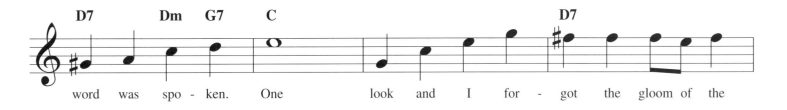

word was spo - ken. One look and I for - got the gloom of the

past. One look and I had found my fu - ture at

last. One look and I had found a world com - plete - ly

new, when love walked in with you. _____

LUCKY TO BE ME
from ON THE TOWN

Words by BETTY COMDEN and ADOLPH GREEN
Music by LEONARD BERNSTEIN

Moderately

What a day, for - tune smiled and came my way,
What a night, sud - den - ly you came in sight,

bring - ing love I nev - er thought I'd see. I'm so luck - y to be
look - ing just the way I'd hoped you'd be. I'm so luck - y to be

1. me.   2. me.   I am sim - ply thun - der - struck

at this change in my luck. Knew at once I want - ed you,

nev - er dreamed you'd want me too. I'm so proud you chose me from

all the crowd. There's no oth - er guy I'd rath - er be, I could

laugh out loud. I'm so luck - y to be me. _____

MOONLIGHT BECOMES YOU
from the Paramount Picture ROAD TO MOROCCO

Words by JOHNNY BURKE
Music by JAMES VAN HEUSEN

LULLABY OF BIRDLAND

Words by GEORGE DAVID WEISS
Music by GEORGE SHEARING

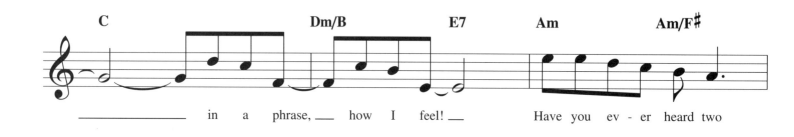

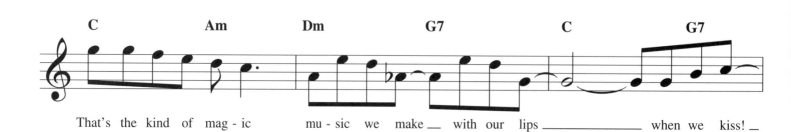

MACK THE KNIFE
from THE THREEPENNY OPERA

English Words by MARC BLITZSTEIN
Original German Words by BERT BRECHT
Music by KURT WEILL

Moderately fast

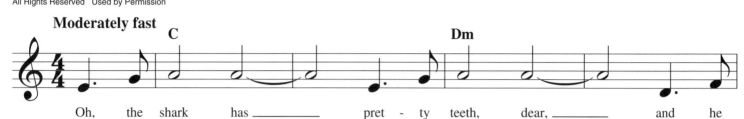

Oh, the shark has pret - ty teeth, dear, and he

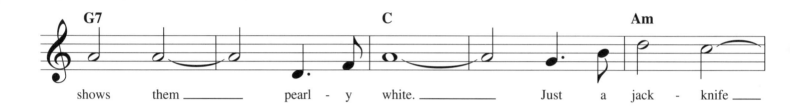

shows them pearl - y white. Just a jack - knife

has Mac - heath, dear, and he keeps it out of

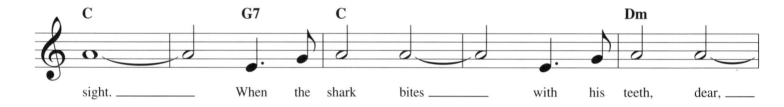

sight. When the shark bites with his teeth, dear,

scar - let bil - lows start to spread. Fan - cy

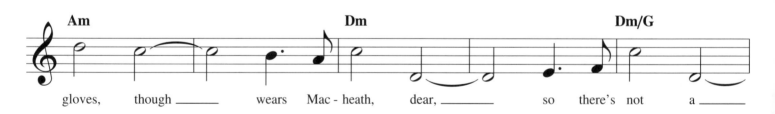

gloves, though wears Mac - heath, dear, so there's not a

trace of red. On the side - walk
Mil - ler

THE MAN I LOVE
from LADY BE GOOD
from STRIKE UP THE BAND

Music and Lyrics by GEORGE GERSHWIN
and IRA GERSHWIN

Moderately

Some - day he'll come a - long, the man I love.

And he'll be big and strong, the man I love. And when he comes my way,

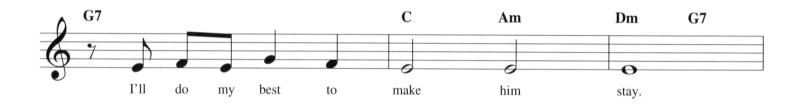

I'll do my best to make him stay.

He'll look at me and smile, I'll un - der - stand, and in a lit - tle while

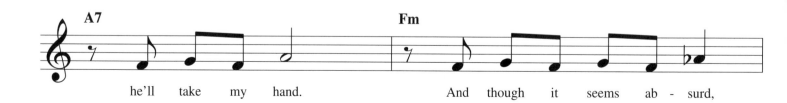

he'll take my hand. And though it seems ab - surd,

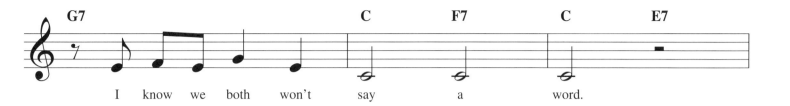

I know we both won't say a word.

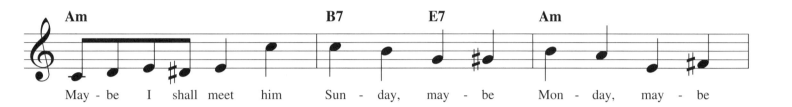

May - be I shall meet him Sun - day, may - be Mon - day, may - be

not. Still I'm sure to meet him one day, may - be

Tues - day will be my good news day. We'll build a lit - tle home,

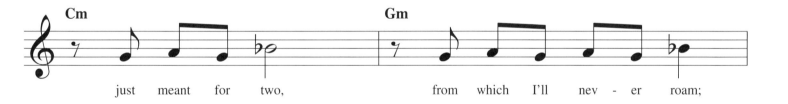

just meant for two, from which I'll nev - er roam;

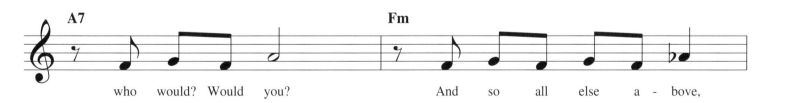

who would? Would you? And so all else a - bove,

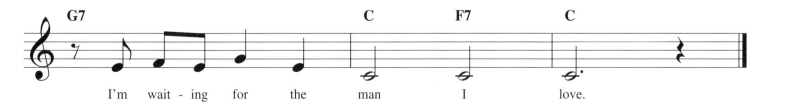

I'm wait - ing for the man I love.

MIDNIGHT SUN

Words and Music by LIONEL HAMPTON,
SONNY BURKE and JOHNNY MERCER

Moderately

Your lips were like a red and ru - by chal - ice, warm - er than the
can't ex - plain the sil - ver rain that found me, or was that a

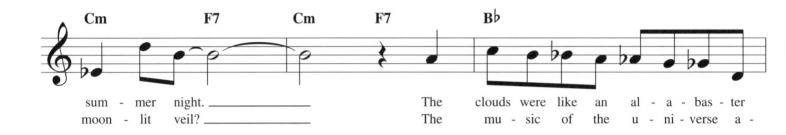

sum - mer night. ____ The clouds were like an al - a - bas - ter
moon - lit veil? ____ The mu - sic of the u - ni - verse a -

pal - ace ris - ing to a snow - y height. ____ Each
round me, or was that a night - in - gale? ____ And

star its own au - ro - ra bo - re - a - lis, sud - den - ly you held me tight. ____
then your arms mir - ac - u - lous - ly found me, sud - den - ly the sky turned pale. ____

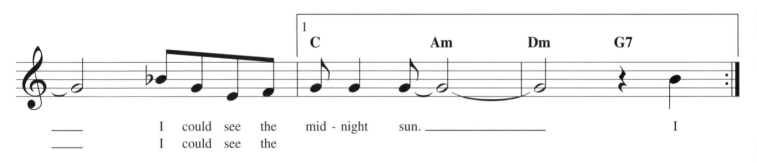

____ I could see the mid - night sun. ____ I
____ I could see the

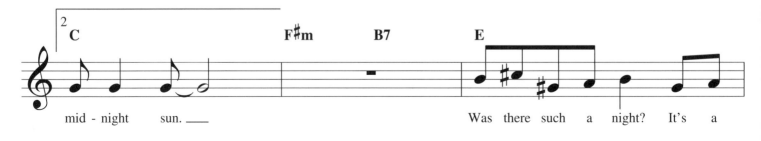

mid - night sun. ____ Was there such a night? It's a

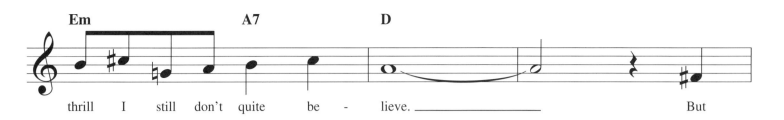
thrill I still don't quite be - lieve. _____ But

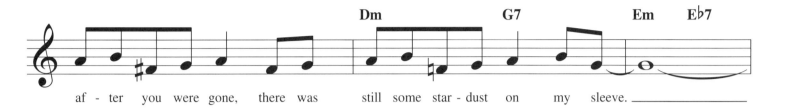
af - ter you were gone, there was still some star - dust on my sleeve. _____

_____ The flame of it may dwin - dle to an em - ber, and the stars for -

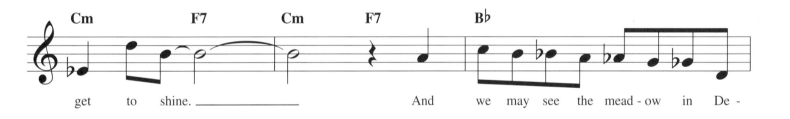
get to shine. _____ And we may see the mead - ow in De -

cem - ber, i - cy white and crys - tal - line. _____ But,

oh, my dar - ling, al - ways I'll re - mem - ber when your lips were close to mine, _____

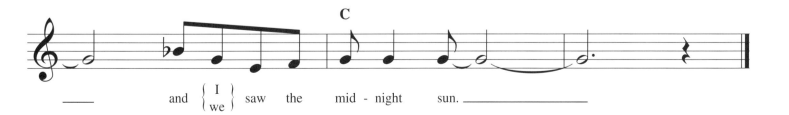
_____ and { I / we } saw the mid - night sun. _____

NICE WORK IF YOU CAN GET IT
from A DAMSEL IN DISTRESS

Music and Lyrics by GEORGE GERSHWIN
and IRA GERSHWIN

Moderately slow

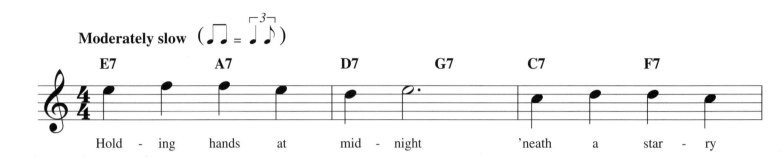

Hold - ing   hands   at   mid - night   'neath   a   star - ry

sky,   nice   work __ if   you   can   get   it,   and   you   can

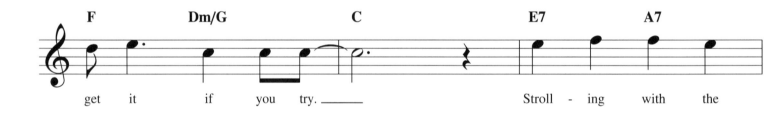

get   it   if   you   try. ____   Stroll - ing   with   the

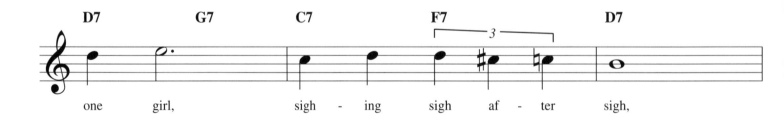

one   girl,   sigh - ing   sigh   af - ter   sigh,

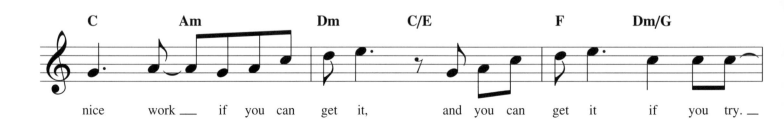

nice   work __ if   you   can   get   it,   and   you   can   get   it   if   you   try. __

113

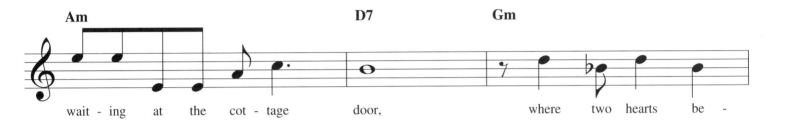

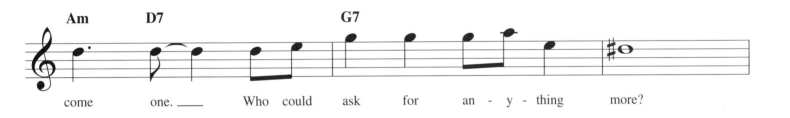

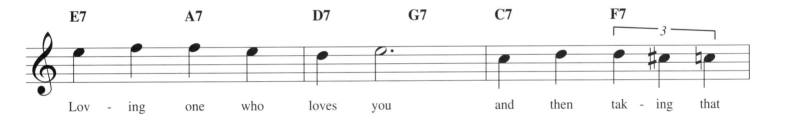

NIGHT AND DAY
from THE GAY DIVORCE

Words and Music by
COLE PORTER

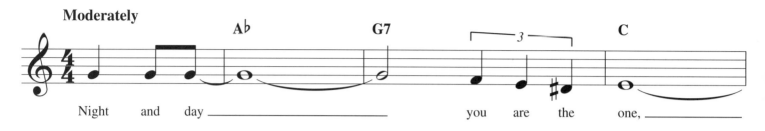

Night and day _____ you are the one, ____

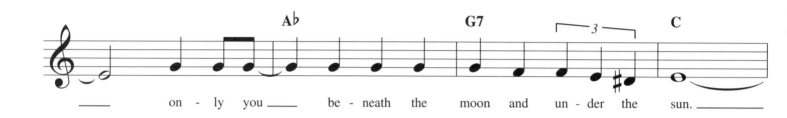

____ on - ly you ____ be - neath the moon and un - der the sun. ____

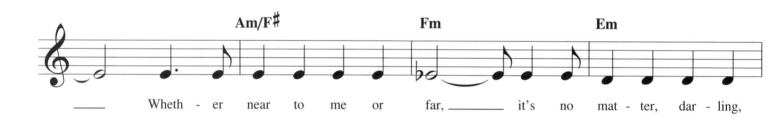

____ Wheth - er near to me or far, ____ it's no mat - ter, dar - ling,

where you are. ____ I think of you _____ night and day. ____

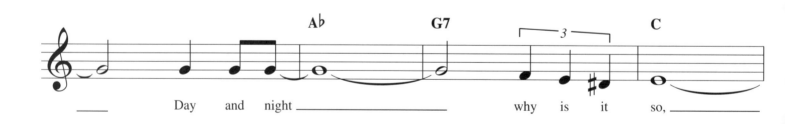

____ Day and night _____ why is it so, ____

____ that this long - ing for you fol - lows wher - ev - er I go? ____

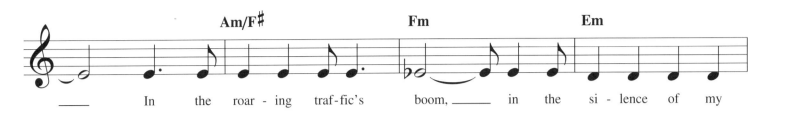

In the roar-ing traf-fic's boom, ____ in the si-lence of my

lone-ly room, _ I think of you ____ night and day. ____

____ Night and day, ____ un-der the hide of me, ____

____ there's an, oh, such a hun-gry yearn - ing burn - ing in -

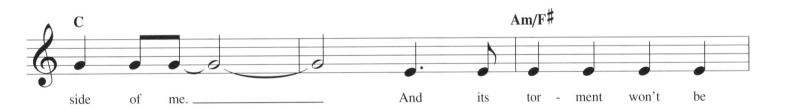

side of me. ____ And its tor - ment won't be

through ____ 'til you let me spend my life mak-ing love _ to you,

day and night, ____ night and day. ____

NUAGES

By DJANGO REINHARDT
and JACQUES LARUE

ON GREEN DOLPHIN STREET
Theme of the MGM Picture GREEN DOLPHIN STREET

Lyrics by NED WASHINGTON
Music by BRONISLAU KAPER

ONCE IN A WHILE

Words by BUD GREEN
Music by MICHAEL EDWARDS

Moderately

OVER THE RAINBOW
from THE WIZARD OF OZ

Music by HAROLD ARLEN
Lyric by E.Y. "YIP" HARBURG

Moderately

Some - where o - ver the rain - bow way up high, there's a
Some - where o - ver the rain - bow skies are blue, and the

land that I heard of once in a lull - a - by.
dreams that you dare to dream real - ly do come true. Some-

day I'll wish up - on a star and wake up where the clouds are far be - hind me.

Where trou - bles melt like lem - on drops, a - way, a - bove the chim - ney tops that's

where you'll find me. Some - where o - ver the rain - bow blue - birds fly.

Birds fly o - ver the rain - bow, why then, oh why can't I? (Instrumental)

If

hap - py lit - tle blue - birds fly be - yond the rain - bow, why, oh why can't I?

PIECES OF DREAMS
(Little Boy Lost)
from the Motion Picture PIECES OF DREAMS

Lyrics by ALAN and MARILYN BERGMAN
Music by MICHEL LEGRAND

Moderately

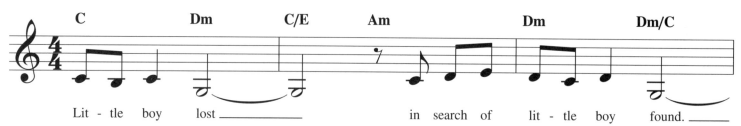

Lit - tle boy lost _____ in search of lit - tle boy found. _____

_____ You go a - won - der - ing, wan - der - ing, stum - bl - ing, tum - bl - ing,

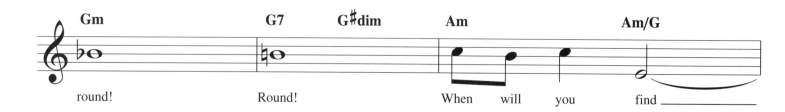

round! Round! When will you find _____

_____ what's on the tip of your mind? _____

Why are you blind _____ to all you ev - er were, nev - er were,

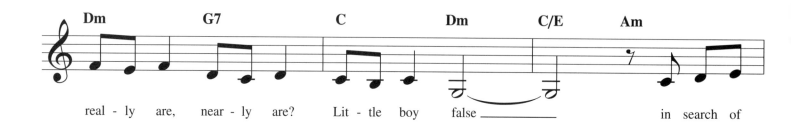

real - ly are, near - ly are? Lit - tle boy false _____ in search of

121

PUT ON A HAPPY FACE
from BYE BYE BIRDIE

Lyric by LEE ADAMS
Music by CHARLES STROUSE

Lightly

Gray skies are gon - na clear up, _____ put on a hap - py

face. Brush off the clouds and cheer up, _____

put on a hap - py face. Take off the gloom - y

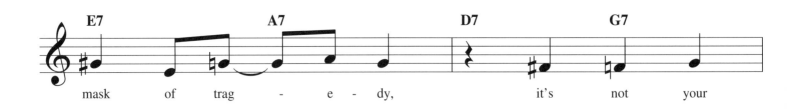

mask of trag - e - dy, it's not your

style. You'll look so good that you'll be glad ___ ya' de -

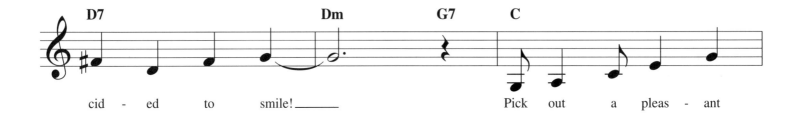

cid - ed to smile! ___ Pick out a pleas - ant

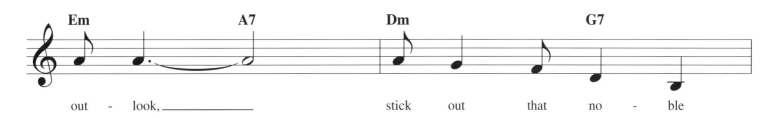

out - look,_____ stick out that no - ble

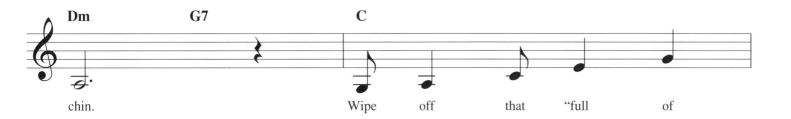

chin. Wipe off that "full of

doubt" look,_____ slap on a hap - py

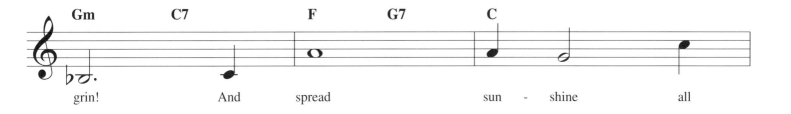

grin! And spread sun - shine all

o - ver the place, just put on a

hap - py face!_____

SECRET LOVE

Words by PAUL FRANCIS WEBSTER
Music by SAMMY FAIN

Moderately

Once   I   had   a   se - cret   love _____   that   lived   with - in   the   heart   of
So   I   told   a   friend - ly   star, _____   the   way   that   dream - ers   of - ten

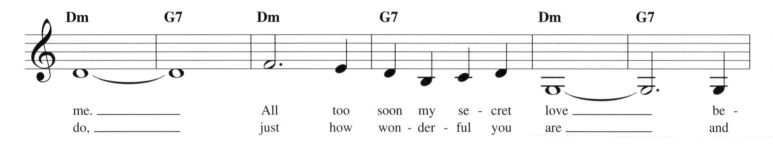

me. _____   All   too   soon   my   se - cret   love _____   be -
do, _____   just   how   won - der - ful   you   are _____   and

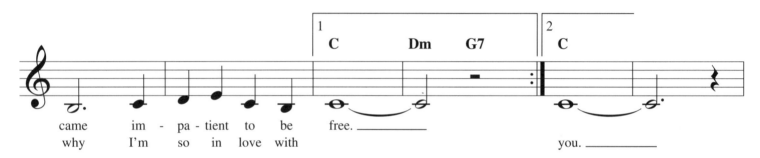

came   im - pa - tient   to   be   free. _____
why   I'm   so   in   love   with   you. _____

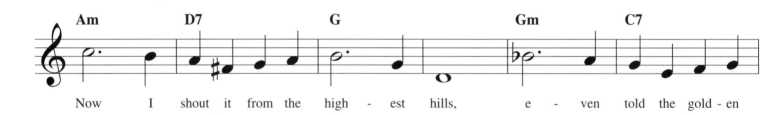

Now   I   shout   it   from   the   high - est   hills,   e - ven   told   the   gold - en

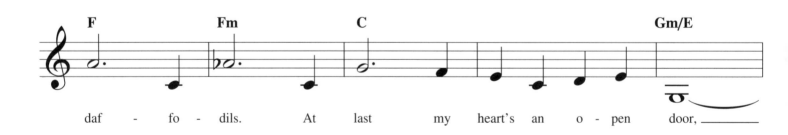

daf - fo - dils.   At   last   my   heart's   an   o - pen   door, _____

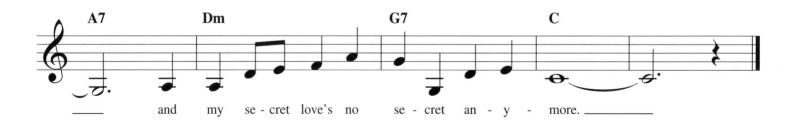

_____   and   my   se - cret   love's   no   se - cret   an - y - more. _____

SEPTEMBER IN THE RAIN

Words by AL DUBIN
Music by HARRY WARREN

THE SHADOW OF YOUR SMILE
Love Theme from THE SANDPIPER

Music by JOHNNY MANDEL
Words by PAUL FRANCIS WEBSTER

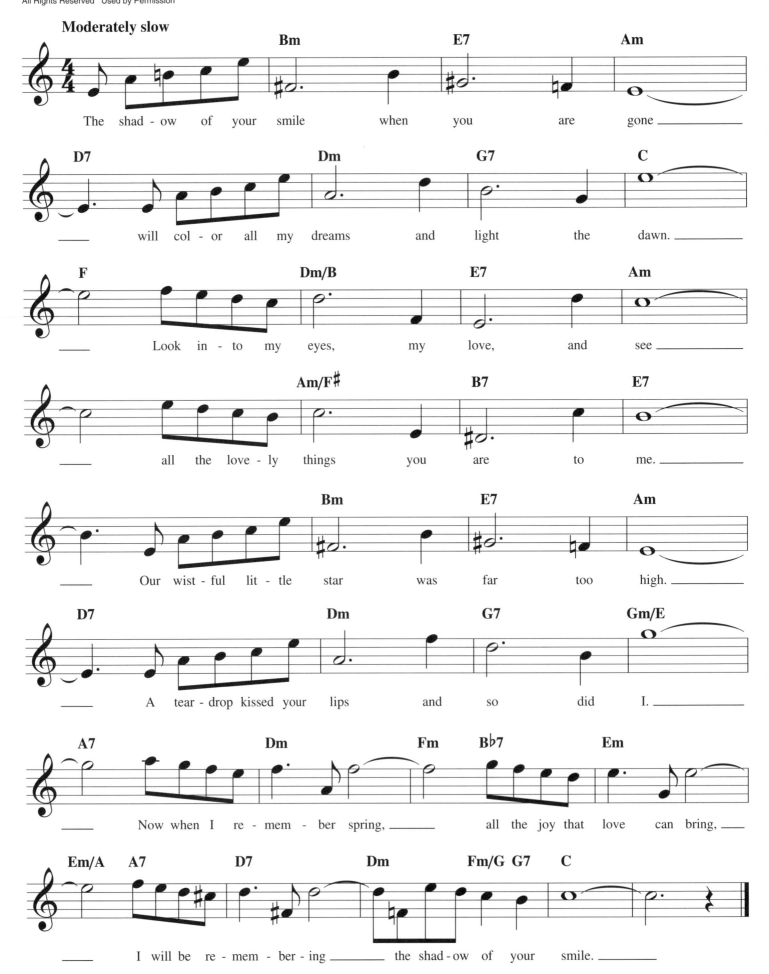

SOME OTHER TIME
from ON THE TOWN

Lyrics by BETTY COMDEN and ADOLPH GREEN
Music by LEONARD BERNSTEIN

SOMEONE TO WATCH OVER ME
from OH, KAY!

Music and Lyrics by GEORGE GERSHWIN
and IRA GERSHWIN

SPRING IS HERE
from I MARRIED AN ANGEL

Words by LORENZ HART
Music by RICHARD RODGERS

SWEET GEORGIA BROWN

Words and Music by BEN BERNIE,
MACEO PINKARD and KENNETH CASEY

No gal made ___ has got a shade ___ on sweet Geor - gia Brown, ___

___ two left feet ___ but oh so neat ___ has

sweet Geor - gia Brown. ___ They all sigh ___ and

wan - na die ___ for sweet Geor - gia Brown. ___ I'll tell ___ you just

why, ___ you know ___ I don't lie, not

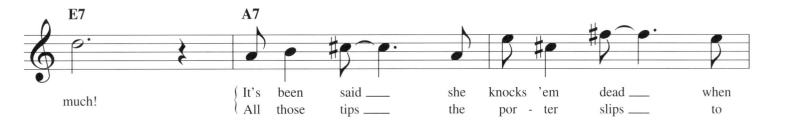

much!

It's been said ___ she knocks 'em dead ___ when
All those tips ___ the por - ter slips ___ to

she lands in town. ___ Since she came ___ why
sweet Geor - gia Brown, ___ they buy clothes ___ at

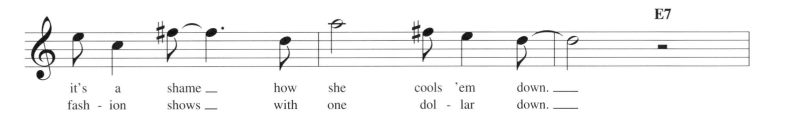

it's a shame ___ how she cools 'em down. ___
fash - ion shows ___ with one dol - lar down. ___

Fel - lers ___ she can't get ___ are fel - lers ___
Oh boy, ___ tip your hats, ___ oh joy, ___

she ain't met. ___ Geor - gia claimed her, Geor - gia named ___ her
she's the "cat's." ___ Who's that, mis - ter, 'tain't her sis - ter,

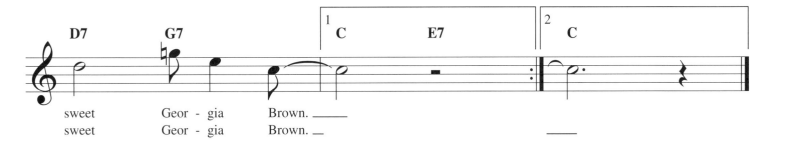

sweet Geor - gia Brown. ___
sweet Geor - gia Brown. ___   ___

TEA FOR TWO
from NO, NO, NANETTE

Words by IRVING CAESAR
Music by VINCENT YOUMANS

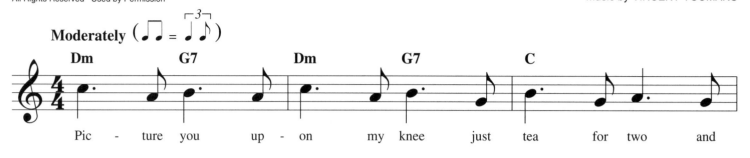

Pic - ture you up - on my knee just tea for two and

two for tea, just me for you and you for me a-

lone. _____ No - bod - y near us to

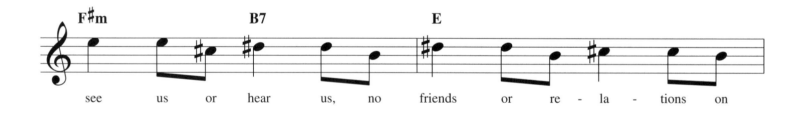

see us or hear us, no friends or re - la - tions on

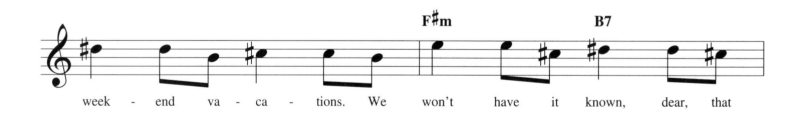

week - end va - ca - tions. We won't have it known, dear, that

we own a tel - e - phone, dear.

Day will break and you'll a - wake and start to bake a

sug - ar cake for me to take for all the boys to

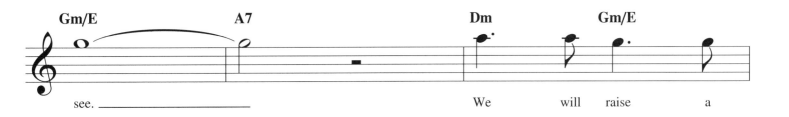

see. _____ We will raise a

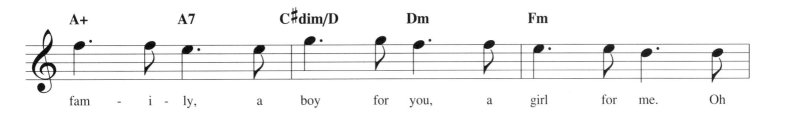

fam - i - ly, a boy for you, a girl for me. Oh

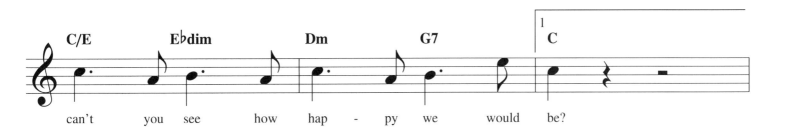

can't you see how hap - py we would be?

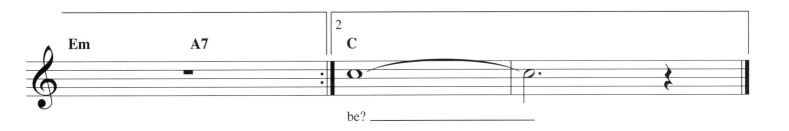

be? _____

THESE FOOLISH THINGS
(Remind Me of You)

Words by HOLT MARVELL
Music by JACK STRACHEY

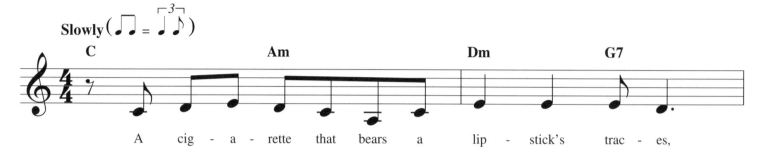

A cig-a-rette that bears a lip-stick's trac-es,

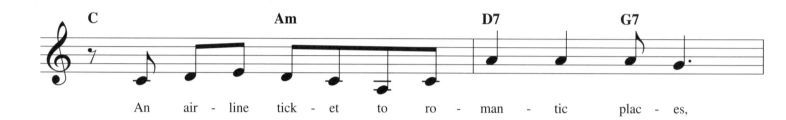

An air-line tick-et to ro-man-tic plac-es,

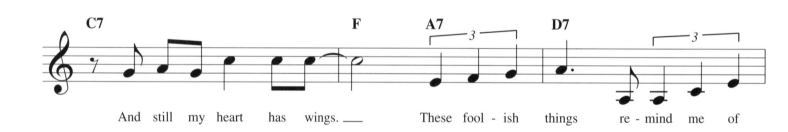

And still my heart has wings. ___ These fool-ish things re-mind me of

you. A tin-kling pia-no in the next a-part-ment,

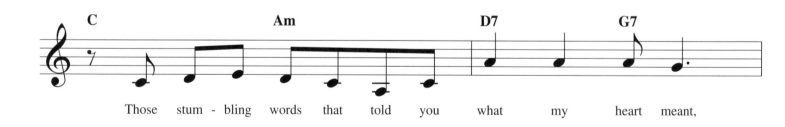

Those stum-bling words that told you what my heart meant,

A fair-ground's paint-ed swings, ___ these fool-ish

A TIME FOR LOVE
from AN AMERICAN DREAM

Music by JOHNNY MANDEL
Words by PAUL FRANCIS WEBSTER

Slowly

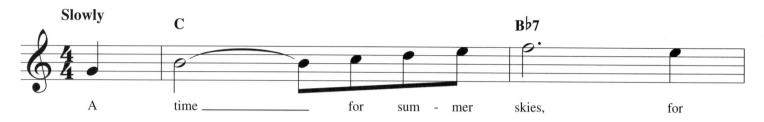

A time _____ for sum - mer skies, for

hum - ming - birds and but - ter - flies, for ten - der words that

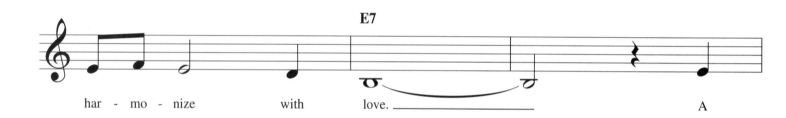

har - mo - nize with love. _____ A

time _____ for climb - ing hills, for lean - ing out of

win - dow sills ad - mir - ing the daf - fo - dils a -

bove. _____ A time for hold - ing hands to -

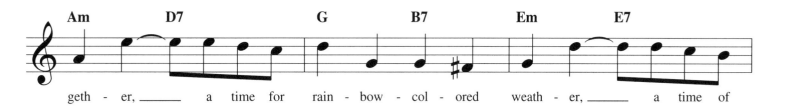

geth - er, _____ a time for rain - bow - col - ored weath - er, _____ a time of

make be - lieve that we've been dream - ing of. _____

_____ As time _____ goes drift - ing by, the

wil - low bends and so do I. But, oh, my friends, what -

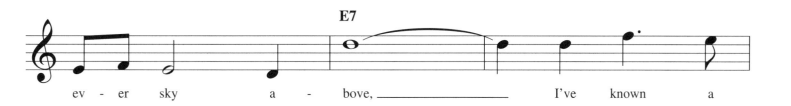

ev - er sky a - bove, _____ I've known a

time for spring, a time for fall, but best of all a

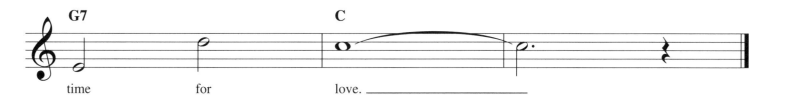

time for love. _____

THE TROLLEY SONG
from MEET ME IN ST. LOUIS

Words and Music by HUGH MARTIN
and RALPH BLANE

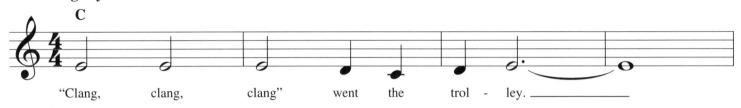

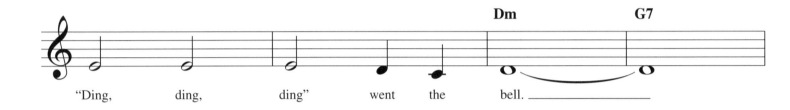

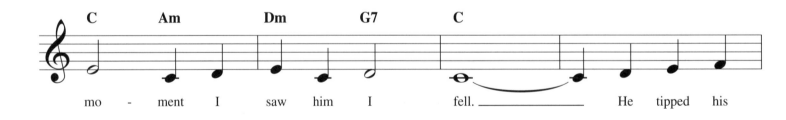

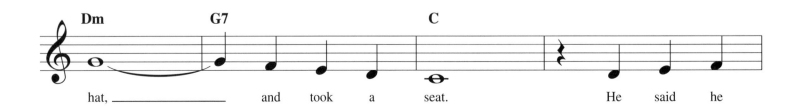

hoped he had - n't stepped up - on my feet. He asked my

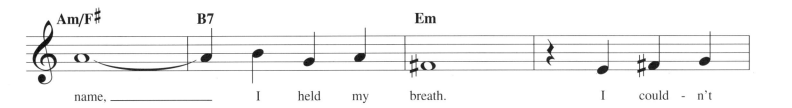

name, _____ I held my breath. I could - n't

speak be - cause he scared me half to death. _____

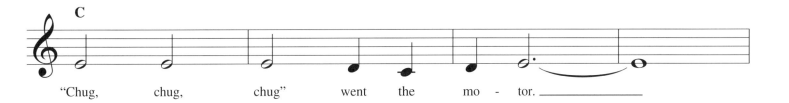

"Chug, chug, chug" went the mo - tor. _____

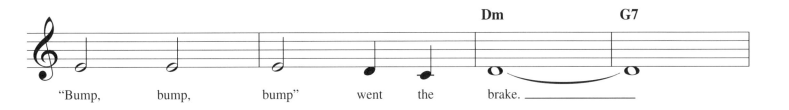

"Bump, bump, bump" went the brake. _____

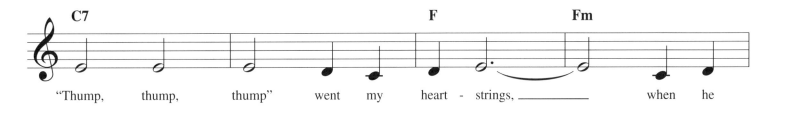

"Thump, thump, thump" went my heart - strings, _____ when he

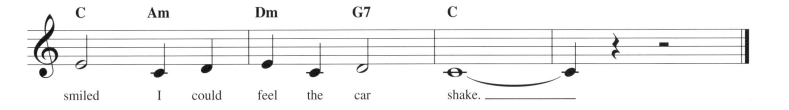

smiled I could feel the car shake. _____

UNFORGETTABLE

Words and Music by
IRVING GORDON

WHAT IS THIS THING CALLED LOVE?
from WAKE UP AND DREAM

Words and Music by
COLE PORTER

WHAT ARE YOU DOING THE REST OF YOUR LIFE?
from THE HAPPY ENDING

Lyrics by ALAN and MARILYN BERGMAN
Music by MICHEL LEGRAND

Moderately, with feeling

What are you do-ing the rest of your life, _____ north and south and east and
times of your days, _____ all the nick-els and the

west of your life? _____ I have on-ly one re-quest of your life: _____
dimes of your days, _____ let the rea-sons and the rhymes of your days _____

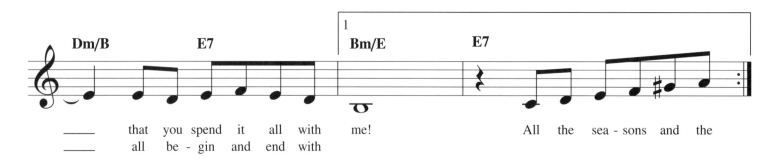

that you spend it all with me! All the sea-sons and the
all be-gin and end with

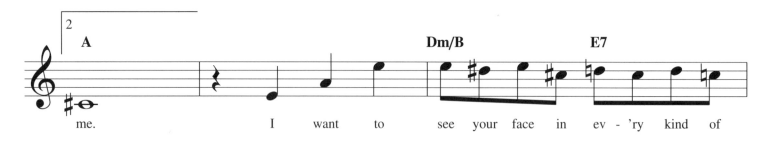

me. I want to see your face in ev-'ry kind of

light, in fields of dawn and for-ests of the night. And when you

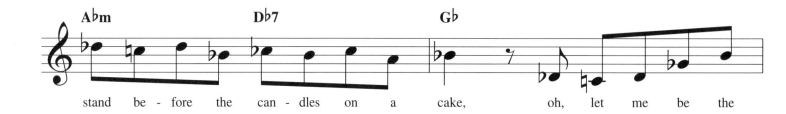

stand be-fore the can-dles on a cake, oh, let me be the

143

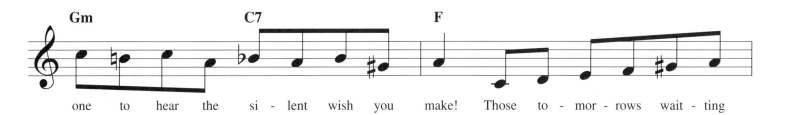
one to hear the si - lent wish you make! Those to - mor - rows wait - ting

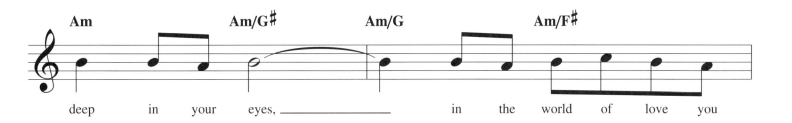
deep in your eyes, _____ in the world of love you

keep in your eyes, _____ I'll a - wak - en what's a - sleep in your eyes. _____

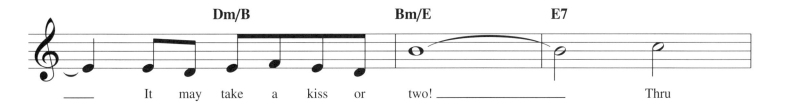
_____ It may take a kiss or two! _____ Thru

all of my life, _____ sum - mer, win - ter, spring and fall of my life, _____

_____ all I ev - er will re - call of my life is

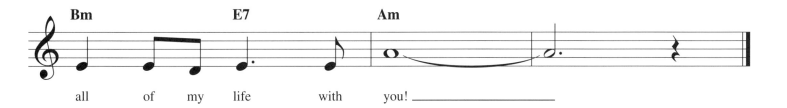
all of my life with you! _____

WHEN SUNNY GETS BLUE

Lyric by JACK SEGAL
Music by MARVIN FISHER

Slow Blues tempo

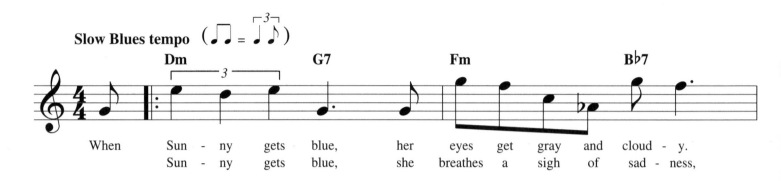

When   Sun - ny   gets   blue,   her   eyes   get   gray   and   cloud - y.
Sun - ny   gets   blue,   she   breathes   a   sigh   of   sad - ness,

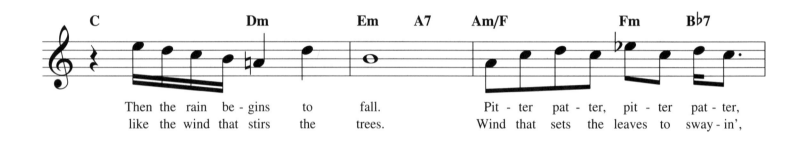

Then   the   rain   be - gins   to   fall.   Pit - ter   pat - ter,   pit - ter   pat - ter,
like   the   wind   that   stirs   the   trees.   Wind   that   sets   the   leaves   to   sway - in',

love   is   gone,   so   what   can   mat - ter?   No   sweet   lov - er   man   comes   to
like   some   vi - o - lins   are   play - in'   weird   and   haunt - ing   mel - o -

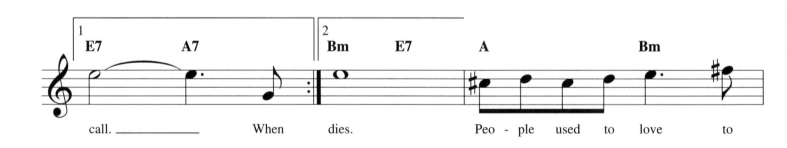

call. _____   When   dies.   Peo - ple   used   to   love   to

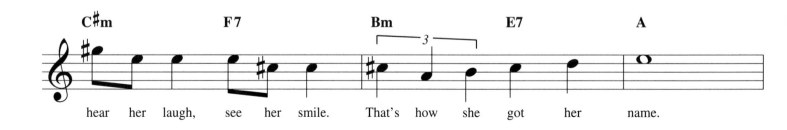

hear   her   laugh,   see   her   smile.   That's   how   she   got   her   name.

145

Since that sad af - fair, she's lost her smile, changed her style. Some - how she's not the

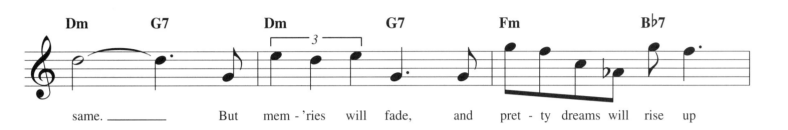

same. _____ But mem - 'ries will fade, and pret - ty dreams will rise up

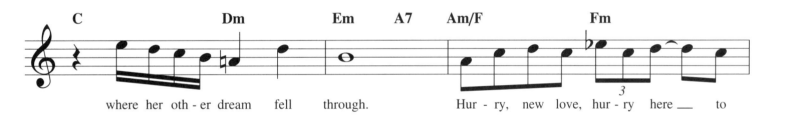

where her oth - er dream fell through. Hur - ry, new love, hur - ry here __ to

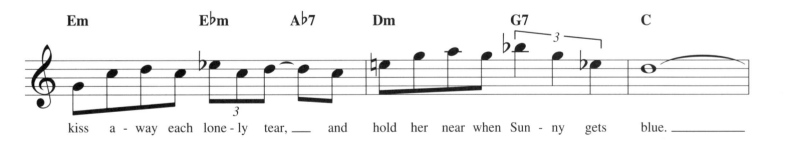

kiss a - way each lone - ly tear, __ and hold her near when Sun - ny gets blue. _____

_____ Hold her near when Sun - ny gets blue. _____

WHEN YOUR LOVER HAS GONE

Words and Music by
E.A. SWAN

Moderately

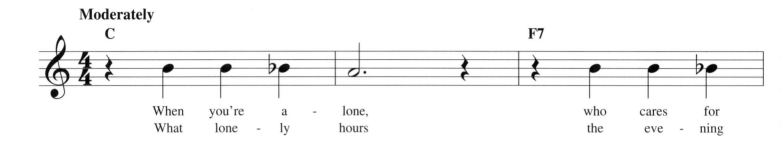

When you're a - lone,   who cares for
What lone - ly hours   the eve - ning

star - lit skies?   When you're a - lone,
shad - ows bring.   What lone - ly hours,

the mag - ic moon - light dies.   At break of dawn,
with mem - 'ries lin - ger - ing.   Like fad - ed flow'rs,

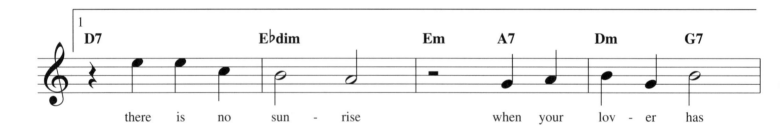

there is no sun - rise   when your lov - er has

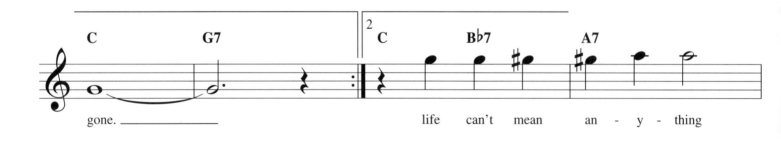

gone.   life can't mean an - y - thing

when your lov - er has gone.

WHERE DO YOU START?

Music by JOHNNY MANDEL
Words and Music by ALAN and MARILYN BERGMAN

Slowly, freely

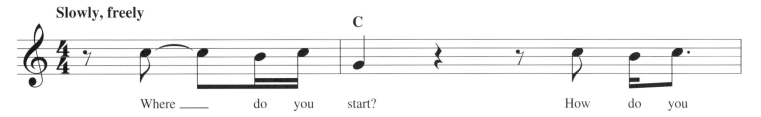

Where ___ do you start? How do you

sep-a-rate the pres-ent from the past? How do you

deal with all the things you thought would last, that did-n't

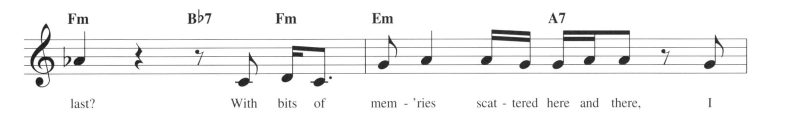

last? With bits of mem-'ries scat-tered here and there, I

look a-round and don't know where to start.

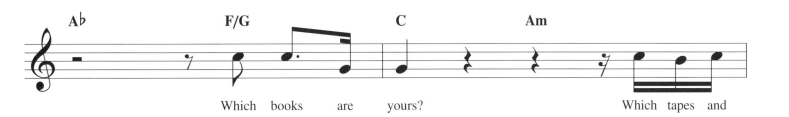

Which books are yours? Which tapes and

WILLOW WEEP FOR ME

Words and Music by
ANN RONELL

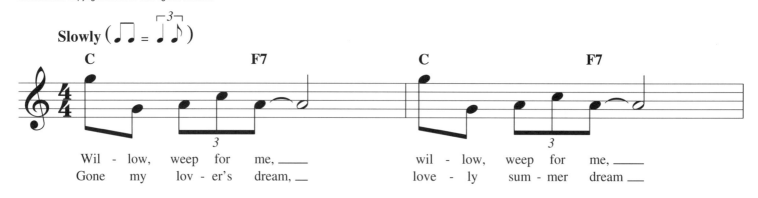

Wil - low, weep for me, _____ wil - low, weep for me, _____
Gone my lov - er's dream, _ love - ly sum - mer dream _

bend your branch - es green, _ a - long the stream _ that runs to sea. _____
gone and left me here _ to weep my tears _____ in - to the stream. _

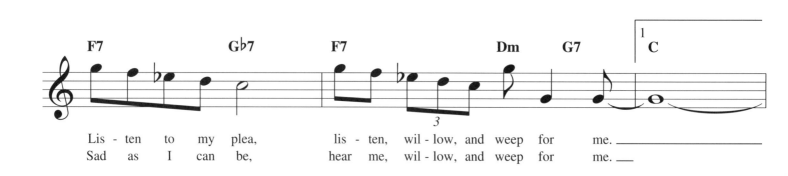

Lis - ten to my plea, lis - ten, wil - low, and weep for me. _____
Sad as I can be, hear me, wil - low, and weep for me. _

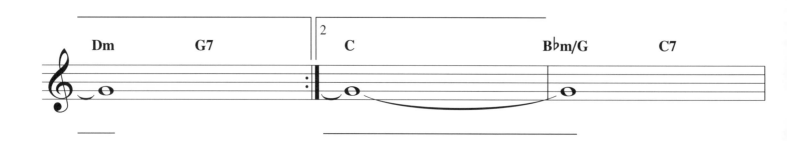

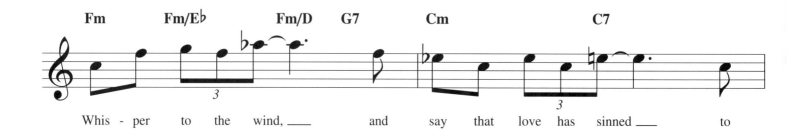

Whis - per to the wind, _____ and say that love has sinned _____ to

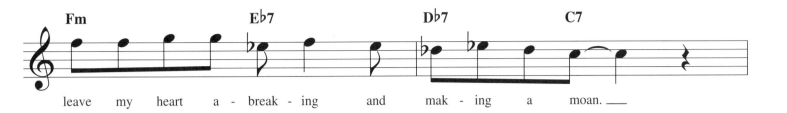

leave my heart a - break - ing and mak - ing a moan. ___

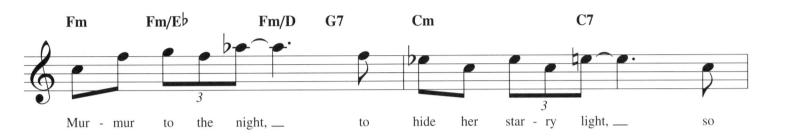

Mur - mur to the night, ___ to hide her star - ry light, ___ so

none will find me sigh - ing and cry - ing all a - lone. ___ Oh,

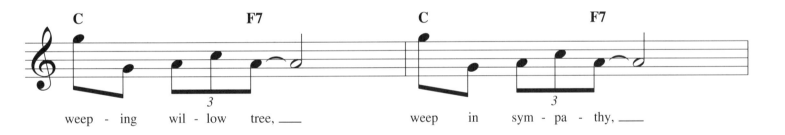

weep - ing wil - low tree, ___ weep in sym - pa - thy, ___

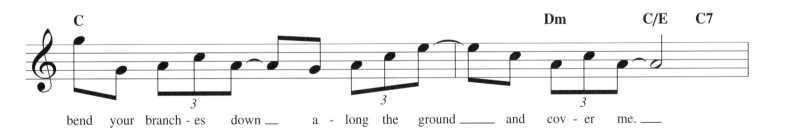

bend your branch - es down ___ a - long the ground ___ and cov - er me. ___

When the shad - ows fall, bend, oh wil - low, and weep for me. ___

YOU DO SOMETHING TO ME
from CAN-CAN

Words and Music by
COLE PORTER

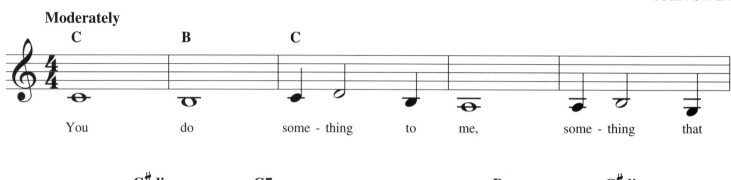

You do some-thing to me, some-thing that

sim - ply mys - ti - fies me. Tell me,

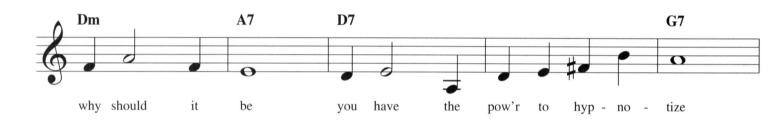

why should it be you have the pow'r to hyp - no - tize

me? Let me live 'neath your spell,

do do ___ that voo - doo ___ that you do ___ so

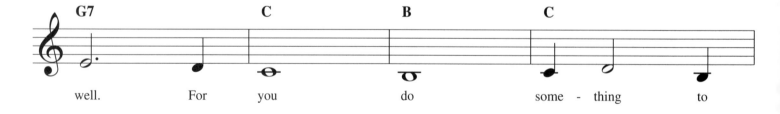

well. For you do some - thing to

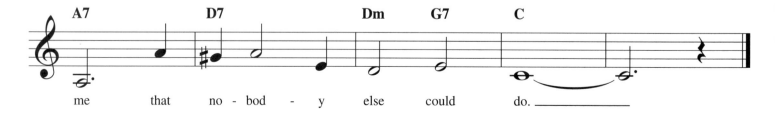

me that no - bod - y else could do. _____

YOU STEPPED OUT OF A DREAM

Words by GUS KAHN
Music by NACIO HERB BROWN

YOU MAKE ME FEEL SO YOUNG
from the 20th Century-Fox Musical THREE LITTLE GIRLS IN BLUE

Words by MACK GORDON
Music by JOSEF MYROW

You make me feel so young, ___ you make me feel like
The mo-ment that you speak, ___ I wan-na go play

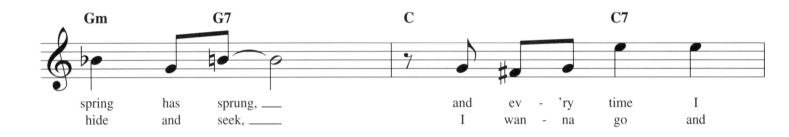

spring has sprung, ___ and ev-'ry time I
hide and seek, ___ I wan-na go and

see you grin, ___ I'm such ___ a hap-py in-di-vid-u-al.
bounce the moon, ___ just like ___

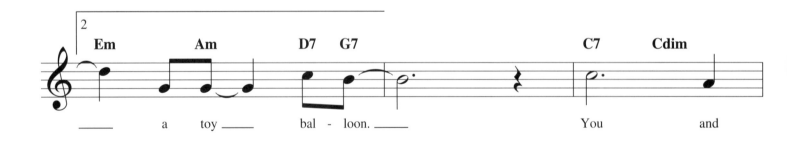

___ a toy ___ bal-loon. ___ You and

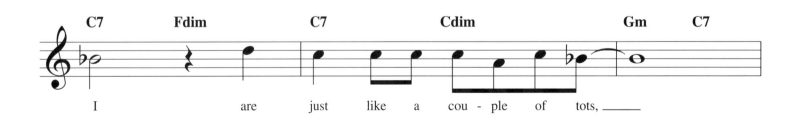

I are just like a cou-ple of tots, ___

155

run - ning a - cross a mead - ow, ___ pick - ing up lots ___ of for -

get - me - nots. ___ You make me feel so young, ___

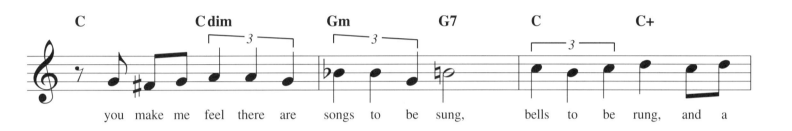

you make me feel there are songs to be sung, bells to be rung, and a

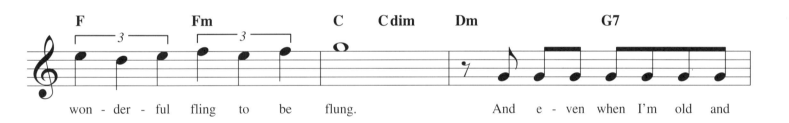

won - der - ful fling to be flung. And e - ven when I'm old and

gray, I'm gon - na feel the way I do to - day, 'cause

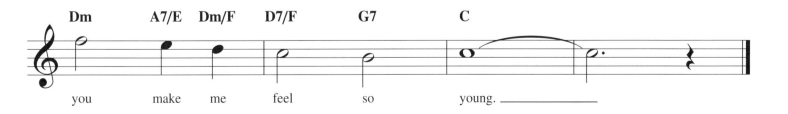

you make me feel so young. _____

CHORD SPELLER

C chords

C	C–E–G
Cm	C–Eb–G
C7	C–E–G–Bb
Cdim	C–Eb–Gb
C+	C–E–G#

C# or Db chords

C#	C#–F–G#
C#m	C#–E–G#
C#7	C#–F– G#–B
C#dim	C#–E–G
C#+	C#–F–A

D chords

D	D–F#–A
Dm	D–F–A
D7	D–F#–A–C
Ddim	D–F–Ab
D+	D–F#–A#

Eb chords

Eb	Eb–G–Bb
Ebm	Eb–Gb–Bb
Eb7	Eb–G–Bb–Db
Ebdim	Eb–Gb–A
Eb+	Eb–G–B

E chords

E	E–G#–B
Em	E–G–B
E7	E–G#–B–D
Edim	E–G–Bb
E+	E–G#–C

F chords

F	F–A–C
Fm	F–Ab–C
F7	F–A–C–Eb
Fdim	F–Ab–B
F+	F–A–C#

F# or Gb chords

F#	F#–A#–C#
F#m	F#–A–C#
F#7	F#–A#–C#–E
F#dim	F#–A–C
F#+	F#–A#–D

G chords

G	G–B–D
Gm	G–Bb–D
G7	G–B–D–F
Gdim	G–Bb–Db
G+	G–B–D#

G# or Ab chords

Ab	Ab–C–Eb
Abm	Ab–B–Eb
Ab7	Ab–C–Eb–Gb
Abdim	Ab–B–D
Ab+	Ab–C–E

A chords

A	A–C#–E
Am	A–C–E
A7	A–C#–E–G
Adim	A–C–Eb
A+	A–C#–F

Bb chords

Bb	Bb–D–F
Bbm	Bb–Db–F
Bb7	Bb–D–F–Ab
Bbdim	Bb–Db–E
Bb+	Bb–D–F#

B chords

B	B–D#–F#
Bm	B–D–F#
B7	B–D#–F#–A
Bdim	B–D–F
B+	B–D#–G

Important Note: A slash chord (C/E, G/B) tells you that a certain bass note is to be played under a particular harmony. In the case of C/E, the chord is C and the bass note is E.

HAL LEONARD PRESENTS
FAKE BOOKS FOR BEGINNERS!

Entry-level fake books! These books feature larger-than-most fake book notation with simplified harmonies and melodies – and all songs are in the key of C. An introduction addresses basic instruction in playing from a fake book.

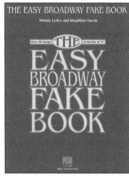

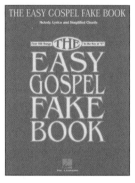

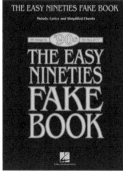

YOUR FIRST FAKE BOOK
00240112...$19.95

THE EASY FAKE BOOK
00240144...$19.95

THE SIMPLIFIED FAKE BOOK
00240168...$19.95

THE BEATLES EASY FAKE BOOK
00240309...$25.00

THE EASY BROADWAY FAKE BOOK
00240180...$19.95

THE EASY CHILDREN'S FAKE BOOK
00240428 ....$19.99

THE EASY CHRISTIAN FAKE BOOK
00240328...$19.99

**THE EASY CHRISTMAS
FAKE BOOK – 2ND EDITION**
00240209...$19.95

THE EASY CLASSIC ROCK FAKE BOOK
00240389 ....$19.99

THE EASY CLASSICAL FAKE BOOK
00240262...$19.95

THE EASY COUNTRY FAKE BOOK
00240319...$19.95

THE EASY DISNEY FAKE BOOK
00240551...$19.99

THE EASY EARLY SONGS FAKE BOOK
00240337 ....$19.99

THE EASY FOLKSONG FAKE BOOK
00240360...$19.99

THE EASY GOSPEL FAKE BOOK
00240169...$19.95

THE EASY HYMN FAKE BOOK
00240207...$19.95

**THE EASY JAZZ STANDARDS
FAKE BOOK**
00102346...$19.99

THE EASY LATIN FAKE BOOK
00240333...$19.99

THE EASY MOVIE FAKE BOOK
00240295...$19.95

THE EASY SHOW TUNES FAKE BOOK
00240297...$19.95

THE EASY STANDARDS FAKE BOOK
00240294...$19.95

THE EASY 3-CHORD FAKE BOOK
00240388 ....$19.99

THE EASY WORSHIP FAKE BOOK
00240265...$19.95

**MORE OF THE EASY WORSHIP
FAKE BOOK**
00240362 ....$19.99

THE EASY TWENTIES FAKE BOOK
00240336 ....$19.99

THE EASY THIRTIES FAKE BOOK
00240335 ....$19.99

THE EASY FORTIES FAKE BOOK
00240252...$19.95

**MORE OF THE EASY
FORTIES FAKE BOOK**
00240287...$19.95

THE EASY FIFTIES FAKE BOOK
00240255...$19.95

**MORE OF THE EASY
FIFTIES FAKE BOOK**
00240288...$19.95

THE EASY SIXTIES FAKE BOOK
00240253...$19.95

**MORE OF THE EASY
SIXTIES FAKE BOOK**
00240289...$19.95

THE EASY SEVENTIES FAKE BOOK
00240256...$19.95

**MORE OF THE EASY SEVENTIES
FAKE BOOK**
00240290...$19.95

THE EASY EIGHTIES FAKE BOOK
00240340 ....$19.99

THE EASY NINETIES FAKE BOOK
00240341 ....$19.99

FOR MORE INFORMATION, SEE YOUR LOCAL MUSIC DEALER,
OR WRITE TO:

HAL•LEONARD®
CORPORATION
7777 W. BLUEMOUND RD. P.O. BOX 13819 MILWAUKEE, WI 53213

www.halleonard.com

Prices, contents and availability subject to change without notice.

THE ULTIMATE COLLECTION OF
FAKE BOOKS

The Real Book – Sixth Edition

Hal Leonard proudly presents the first legitimate and legal editions of these books ever produced. These bestselling titles are mandatory for anyone who plays jazz! Over 400 songs, including: All By Myself • Dream a Little Dream of Me • God Bless the Child • Like Someone in Love • When I Fall in Love • and more.

00240221	Volume 1, C Edition	$35.00
00240224	Volume 1, B♭ Edition	$35.00
00240225	Volume 1, E♭ Edition	$35.00
00240226	Volume 1, BC Edition	$35.00
00240222	Volume 2, C Edition	$35.00
00240227	Volume 2, B♭ Edition	$35.00
00240228	Volume 2, E♭ Edition	$35.00

Best Fake Book Ever – 4th Edition

More than 1,000 songs from all styles of music, including: All My Loving • At the Hop • Cabaret • Dust in the Wind • Fever • From a Distance • Hello, Dolly! • Hey Jude • King of the Road • Longer • Misty • Route 66 • Sentimental Journey • Somebody • Song Sung Blue • Spinning Wheel • Unchained Melody • We Will Rock You • What a Wonderful World • Wooly Bully • Y.M.C.A. • and more.

00290239 C Edition $49.99
00240083 B♭ Edition $49.95
00240084 E♭ Edition $49.95

Classic Rock Fake Book – 2nd Edition

This fake book is a great compilation of more than 250 terrific songs of the rock era, arranged for piano, voice, guitar and all C instruments. Includes: All Right Now • American Woman • Birthday • Honesty • I Shot the Sheriff • I Want You to Want Me • Imagine • It's Still Rock and Roll to Me • Lay Down Sally • Layla • My Generation • Rock and Roll All Nite • Spinning Wheel • White Room • We Will Rock You • lots more!
00240108 ....$32.50

Classical Fake Book – 2nd Edition

This unprecedented, amazingly comprehensive reference includes over 850 classical themes and melodies for all classical music lovers. Includes everything from Renaissance music to Vivaldi and Mozart to Mendelssohn. Lyrics in the original language are included when appropriate.
00240044 ....$37.50

The Disney Fake Book – 3rd Edition

Over 200 of the most beloved songs of all time, including: Be Our Guest • Can You Feel the Love Tonight • Colors of the Wind • Cruella De Vil • Friend Like Me • Heigh-Ho • It's a Small World • Mickey Mouse March • Supercalifragilisticexpialidocious • Under the Sea • When You Wish upon a Star • A Whole New World • Zip-A-... and more!

.................$30.00

...acters and artwork © Disney Enterprises, Inc.)

The Folksong Fake Book

Over 1,000 folksongs perfect for performers, school teachers, and hobbyists. Includes: Bury Me Not on the Lone Prairie • Clementine • Danny Boy • The Erie Canal • Go, Tell It on the Mountain • Home on the Range • Kumbaya • Michael Row the Boat Ashore • Shenandoah • Simple Gifts • Swing Low, Sweet Chariot • When Johnny Comes Marching Home • Yankee Doodle • and many more.
00240151 ....$24.95

The Hymn Fake Book

Nearly 1,000 multi-denominational hymns perfect for church musicians or hobbyists: Amazing Grace • Christ the Lord Is Risen Today • For the Beauty of the Earth • It Is Well with My Soul • A Mighty Fortress Is Our God • O for a Thousand Tongues to Sing • Praise to the Lord, the Almighty • Take My Life and Let It Be • What a Friend We Have in Jesus • and hundreds more!
00240145 ....$24.95

The Praise & Worship Fake Book

400 songs: As the Deer • Better Is One Day • Come, Now Is the Time to Worship • Firm Foundation • Glorify Thy Name • Here I Am to Worship • I Could Sing of Your Love Forever • Lord, I Lift Your Name on High • More Precious Than Silver • Open the Eyes of My Heart • The Power of Your Love • Shine, Jesus, Shine • Trading My Sorrows • We Fall Down • You Are My All in All • and more.
00240234 ....$34.95

The R&B Fake Book – 2nd Edition

This terrific fake book features 375 classic R&B hits: Baby Love • Best of My Love • Dancing in the Street • Easy • Get Ready • Heatwave • Here and Now • Just Once • Let's Get It On • The Loco-Motion • (You Make Me Feel Like) A Natural Woman • One Sweet Day • Papa Was a Rollin' Stone • Save the Best for Last • September • Sexual Healing • Shop Around • Still • Tell It Like It Is • Up on the Roof • Walk on By • What's Going On • more!
00240107 C Edition $29.95

Ultimate Broadway Fake Book – 5th Edition

More than 700 show-stoppers from over 200 shows! Includes: Ain't Misbehavin' • All I Ask of You • Bewitched • Camelot • Don't Cry for Me Argentina • Edelweiss • I Dreamed a Dream • If I Were a Rich Man • Memory • Oklahoma • Send in the Clowns • What I Did for Love • more.
00240046 ....$49.99

FOR MORE INFORMATION, SEE YOUR LOCAL MUSIC DEALER, OR WRITE TO:

HAL•LEONARD® CORPORATION

7777 W. BLUEMOUND RD. P.O. BOX 13819 MILWAUKEE, WI 53213

Complete songlists available online at
www.halleonard.com

Prices, contents and availabilty subject to change without notice.

The Ultimate Christmas Fake Book – 5th Edition

This updated edition includes 275 traditional and contemporary Christmas songs: Away in a Manger • The Christmas Song • Deck the Hall • Frosty the Snow Man • A Holly Jolly Christmas • I Heard the Bells on Christmas Day • Jingle Bells • Little Saint Nick • Merry Christmas, Darling • Nuttin' for Christmas • Rudolph the Red-Nosed Reindeer • Silent Night • What Child Is This? • more.
00240045 ....$24.95

The Ultimate Country Fake Book – 5th Edition

This book includes over 700 of your favorite country hits: Always on My Mind • Boot Scootin' Boogie • Crazy • Down at the Twist and Shout • Forever and Ever, Amen • Friends in Low Places • The Gambler • Jambalaya • King of the Road • Sixteen Tons • There's a Tear in My Beer • Your Cheatin' Heart • and hundreds more.
00240049 ....$49.99

The Ultimate Fake Book – 4th Edition

Includes over 1,200 hits: Blue Skies • Body and Soul • Endless Love • A Foggy Day • Isn't It Romantic? • Memory • Mona Lisa • Moon River • Operator • Piano Man • Roxanne • Satin Doll • Shout • Small World • Speak Softly, Love • Strawberry Fields Forever • Tears in Heaven • Unforgettable • hundreds more!

00240024 C Edition $49.95
00240026 B♭ Edition $49.95
00240025 E♭ Edition $49.95

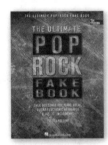

The Ultimate Pop/Rock Fake Book – 4th Edition

Over 600 pop standards and contemporary hits, including: All Shook Up • Another One Bites the Dust • Crying • Don't Know Much • Dust in the Wind • Earth Angel • Every Breath You Take • Hero • Hey Jude • Hold My Hand • Imagine • Layla • The Loco-Motion • Oh, Pretty Woman • On Broadway • Spinning Wheel • Stand by Me • Stayin' Alive • Tears in Heaven • True Colors • The Twist • Vision of Love • A Whole New World • Wild Thing • Wooly Bully • Yesterday • more!
00240099 ....$39.99

Fake Book of the World's Favorite Songs – 4th Edition

Over 700 favorites, including: America the Beautiful • Anchors Aweigh • Battle Hymn of the Republic • Bill Bailey, Won't You Please Come Home • Chopsticks • Für Elise • His Eye Is on the Sparrow • I Wonder Who's Kissing Her Now • Jesu, Joy of Man's Desiring • My Old Kentucky Home • Sidewalks of New York • Take Me Out to the Ball Game • When the Saints Go Marching In • and hundreds more!
00240072 ....$22.95